# 101 Bible Activity Sheets

Reproducible cut-and-paste activities and
puzzle forms for children's church, Sunday schools,
DVBS, and Bible Clubs

## Betty De Vries

## Illustrations by Walter Kerr

Baker Book House

Grand Rapids, Michigan 49506

Materials in this book were taken from the following titles,
copyright 1976-1983 by Baker Book House: *Bible Learn and Do,
Bible Activity Balloon, Bible Puzzle Parade, Bible Puzzle Corral,
Bible Puzzle Basket, Bible Activity Capsule, Bible Puzzle Train,
Christmas Cut-n-Color, Bible Treasures Activity Book, Bible
Puzzle Trails, Bible Puzzle Caravan*

Copyright 1983 by
Baker Book House Company

ISBN: 0-8010-2931-7

*Seventh printing, September 1988*

Printed in the United States of America

# CONTENTS

# Old Testament Stories

# 1. GOD MADE IT

God made all these things on the fourth day of creation.

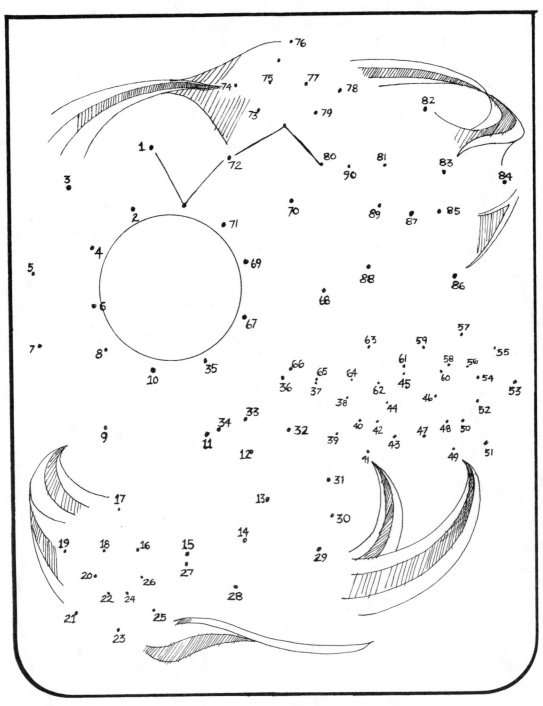

# 2. ANIMAL MOBILE

The Bible talks about many animals. Find the names of the animals mentioned in the following verses. Then color the front and back of each animal. Cut out the pieces and paste them together. Punch out a small hole and put a piece of string through each. Put a knot at the end so that the string cannot slip through the hole. Bend a lightweight coat hanger and hang the animals from it.

I Kings 10:22
_____

Habakkuk 1:8
_____

I Kings 10:25 _____

I Samuel 17:34 _____

Genesis 30:43 _____

Isaiah 11:7 _____

9

# 3. FINGERPRINTS

The Bible talks about many insects and animals. Look up the references below and write in the name of the animal talked about in that Bible verse. Then make some fingerprint animals. We've made a few to show you how. First, press your thumb against an ink pad or color the inside tip of your thumb with a felt-tip marker. Then, press your thumb lightly on the paper to make heads and bodies. Use a pencil or crayon to add legs, ears, mouth, eyes, and whatever else is needed to make the picture complete.

Prov. 6:6-8 _____    Prov. 30:28 _____

Judges 6:5 _____    Lev. 3:7 _____

Lev. 11:29 _____

Ps. 103:21 _____   Lev. 11:29 _____

Ps. 105:34 _____

Judges 14:8 _____   Ps. 105:30 _____

Ps. 104:18 _____

# 4. STACK-A-WORD

All of the words listed below fit into this puzzle, one letter to a square. They are things God made when He created the world. You can read the story in the first book of the Bible, the Book of Genesis.

DAY      LIGHT
MAN     GRASS
SUN      WATER
SEAS    WOMAN
SAND   CATTLE
LAND   WHALES
MOON  SNAKES
ANTS    ANIMALS
FISH    INSECTS
BIRDS  HEAVENS
EARTH  CREATION
STARS  CREATURES
NIGHT

# 5. DOT-TO-DOT

Connect these words (go from one dot to the next) to make the first sentence in the Bible. On which day of creation did God make the object you've drawn? _____

# 6. JUST FOR FUN

To get a message, cross out every third letter.

**ANTDGAODOMANDENTWEOGERETATBLIDGHOTSO,**

**THEEGDRESATKERJLIMGHETTHORAULDETOHESDAEY,**

**AONDCTHOELAESSSEKRLOIGSHTGTORRUSLEDTHU**

**ENAIGNHTO:HEMMAZDEQTHGESFTAIRSEALISO.**

# 7. BIRD MOBILE

The Bible talks about several birds. Find the names of the birds mentioned in the following verses. Then color the front and back of each bird. Cut them out and paste together. Punch out a small hole and put a piece of string through each. Put a knot at the end so that the string cannot slip through the hole. Bend a lightweight coat hanger and hang the birds from it.

Psalm 102:7 _____

Psalm 102:6 _____

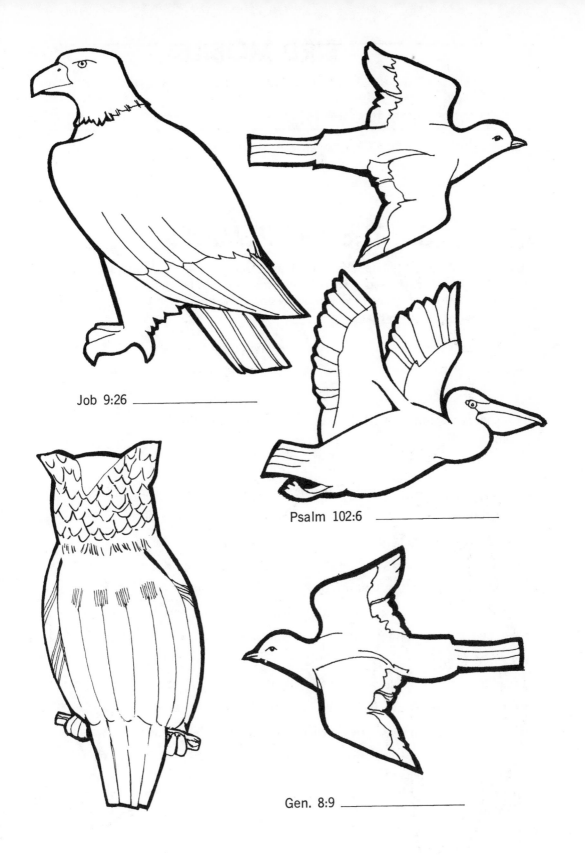

Job 9:26 _____

Psalm 102:6 _____

Gen. 8:9 _____

# 8. THE TEN PLAGUES

Psalm 105:26-45 tells about the Ten Plagues sent to the Egyptians and also about the loving care God gave His children while they journeyed in the wilderness. Fill in the missing words below and then find these objects hidden in the picture on the next page.

He sent Moses his servant; and Aaron whom he had chosen. They shewed signs among them, and wonders in the land of Ham. He sent darkness, and made it dark; and they rebelled not against his word. He turned their waters into blood, and slew their _____. Their land brought forth _____ in abundance, in the chambers of their kings. He spake, and there came divers sorts of _____, and _____ in all their coasts. He gave them _____ for rain, and flaming fire in their land. He smote their _____ also and their _____ _____; and brake the trees of their coasts. He spake, and the _____ came, and _____, and that without number, And did eat up all the _____ in their land, and devoured the fruit of their ground. He smote also all the firstborn in their land, and the chief of all their strength. He brought them forth also with silver and gold: and there was not one feeble person among their tribes. Egypt was glad when they departed; for the fear of them fell upon them. He spread a _____ for a covering; and _____ to give light in the night. The people asked, and he brought _____, and satisfied them with the bread of heaven. He opened the _____, and the waters gushed out; they ran in the dry places like a _____. For he remembered his holy promise . . . Praise ye the Lord.

# 9. TOO MANY FROGS

One of the Ten Plagues was frogs over all the land. There are fifteen frogs hidden in this picture. How many can you find?

# 10. GRASSHOPPERS

Twenty-five grasshoppers are hidden in this picture.
How many can you find?
Read about locusts or grasshoppers in Exodus 10:12-19.

# 11. THE HIGH PRIEST'S CLOTHES

In Exodus 28 God gives some special directions for making clothes for Aaron, the high priest. Color the pieces of his clothes on these pages and when you are finished, you'll know how to color the picture of the high priest on page 17.

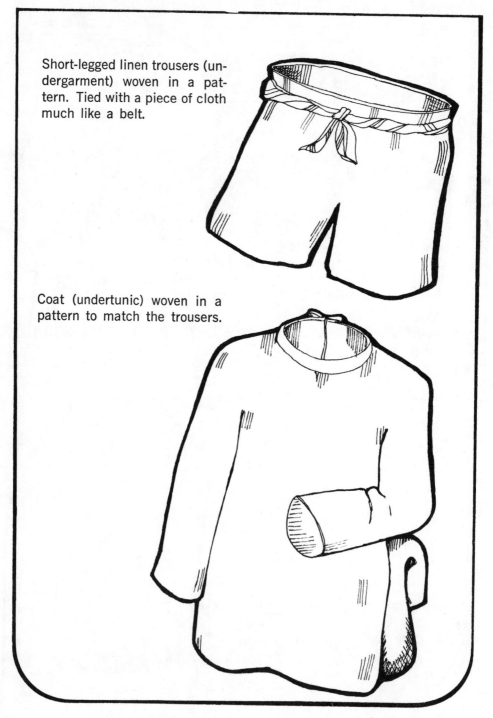

Short-legged linen trousers (undergarment) woven in a pattern. Tied with a piece of cloth much like a belt.

Coat (undertunic) woven in a pattern to match the trousers.

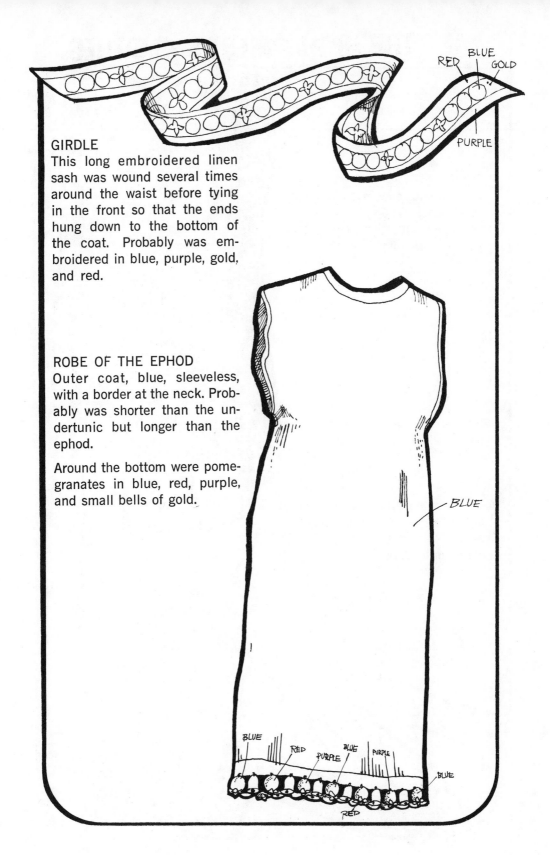

## GIRDLE
This long embroidered linen sash was wound several times around the waist before tying in the front so that the ends hung down to the bottom of the coat. Probably was embroidered in blue, purple, gold, and red.

## ROBE OF THE EPHOD
Outer coat, blue, sleeveless, with a border at the neck. Probably was shorter than the undertunic but longer than the ephod.

Around the bottom were pomegranates in blue, red, purple, and small bells of gold.

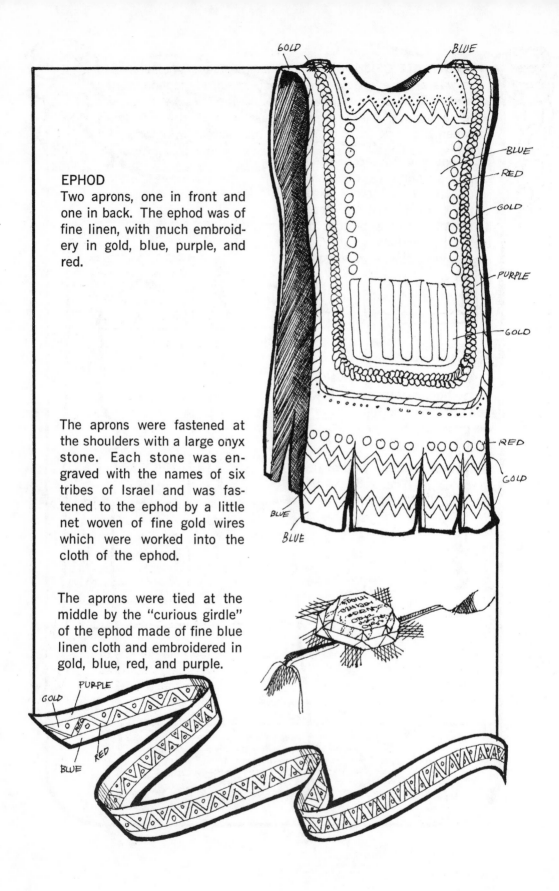

## EPHOD
Two aprons, one in front and one in back. The ephod was of fine linen, with much embroidery in gold, blue, purple, and red.

The aprons were fastened at the shoulders with a large onyx stone. Each stone was engraved with the names of six tribes of Israel and was fastened to the ephod by a little net woven of fine gold wires which were worked into the cloth of the ephod.

The aprons were tied at the middle by the "curious girdle" of the ephod made of fine blue linen cloth and embroidered in gold, blue, red, and purple.

**BREASTPLATE OF JUDGMENT**
This was a piece of fine linen one span wide and two spans long (a span is the distance between the extended thumb and the little finger). The cloth was folded in half to form a square and put inside were the Urim and Thummin*.

The breastplate was fastened to the top of the ephod at the shoulder pieces by rings and chains of gold. It was fastened at the bottom by chains and rings of gold with a lace or tie of blue.

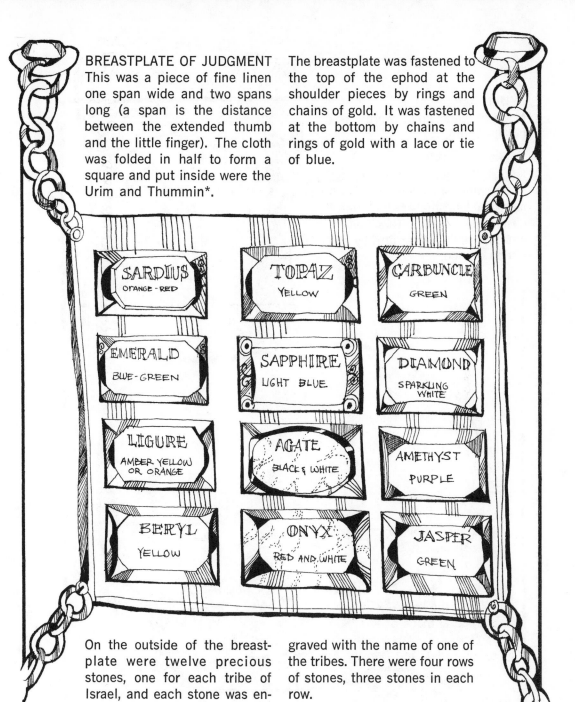

SARDIUS
ORANGE - RED

TOPAZ
YELLOW

CARBUNCLE
GREEN

EMERALD
BLUE-GREEN

SAPPHIRE
LIGHT BLUE

DIAMOND
SPARKLING WHITE

LIGURE
AMBER YELLOW OR ORANGE

AGATE
BLACK & WHITE

AMETHYST
PURPLE

BERYL
YELLOW

ONYX
RED AND WHITE

JASPER
GREEN

On the outside of the breastplate were twelve precious stones, one for each tribe of Israel, and each stone was engraved with the name of one of the tribes. There were four rows of stones, three stones in each row.

*Not everyone agrees on what the Urim and Thummin were. Look them up in a good Bible dictionary or ask your minister or teacher to explain what these words mean.

## SKULL CAP
Made of white linen, worn under the mitre.

## MITRE OR TURBAN
Made of fine linen. On the front of the mitre was a golden plate inscribed with the words "Holiness to the Lord." This plate was fastened to the mitre by a ribbon of blue.

# 12. CLIMBING THROUGH THE JORDAN VALLEY

All of the words in this puzzle are names of men mentioned in the Old Testament. The last letter of each name is the same as the first letter of the next name. Most of these men lived in or near the Jordan Valley and probably climbed the cliffs and hills and scrambled over the rocks on the valley floor.

Here's help with the first two names: ArDan. Now you're on your own. See how many names you can fill in without looking up the Bible reference.

1.  Grandson of Benjamin (Gen. 46:21)   ARD
2.  Son of Jacob (Gen. 30:5)   DAN
3.  A Syrian general healed of leprosy   (II Kings 5)
4.  Sixth son of Jacob (Gen. 30:8)
5.  Ninth son of Jacob   (Gen. 30:18)
6.  Jacob's oldest son (Gen. 29:32)
7.  Builder of the ark (Gen. 6:14)
8.  Son of Dan   (Gen. 46:23)
9.  Oldest son of Joseph (Gen. 41:51)
10. One of the Minor Prophets
11. Son of Abraham (Gen. 21:3)
12. Son of Reuben (Gen. 46:9)
13. First son of Abraham (Gen. 16:15)
14. Abraham's nephew (Gen. 11:31)
15. Son of Issachar (Gen. 46:13)
16. Brother of Cain (Gen. 4)
17. Noah's father (Gen. 5:30)
18. A son of Noah (Gen. 5:32)
19. The oldest man who ever lived (Gen. 5:21)
20. First of the Minor Prophets
21. Brother of Moses (Exod. 7:7)
22. Father of Joshua (Josh. 1:1)
23. A cupbearer (Neh. 1:11)
24. One of Ephraim's sons (I Chron. 27:20)
25. King of Judah (II Chron. 14:1)
26. Father of many nations (Gen. 12:1, 2)
27. Great leader (Exod. 3)
28. The last of Israel's judges (I Chron. 6:26)
29. Father-in-law of Jacob (Gen. 29)
30. Prophet who rebuked David (II Sam. 12:15)
31. A Minor Prophet
32. Son of Lot (Gen. 19:37)
33. Ancestor of David (Ruth 2)

# 13. GIDEON'S ARMY

In the Book of Judges (chapters 6, 7, 8) is the story of Gideon and how he won a battle over the enemies of Israel. Read the story and fill in the blanks below. Then in the big picture find little pictures of the words you have filled in.

There were so many enemies that they seemed to be like _____

in the valley. They had so many _____ that the Israelites couldn't begin to

count them. God told Gideon to use only three hundred men to fight that large army.

Gideon chose his men by watching how they drank water from the stream. Every man

who lapped water like a _____ was chosen to be one of Gideon's men. Their

weapons were a _____ , an empty _____ , and a

_____. All the soldiers were told to shout, "The_____

of the Lord and Gideon." God was with Gideon and his men. The Israelites won the

battle.

What did the angel of the Lord say to Gideon at the winepress? Unscramble the let-

ters below.

**EHT DRLO SI HIWT EHTE, UHOT GHYMTI AMN FO URVOLA.**

_____

# 14. PICTURE PUZZLE

Can you fill in the squares below, using the first letter of each object above the square? When you are finished, you will have written two of the Ten Commandments.

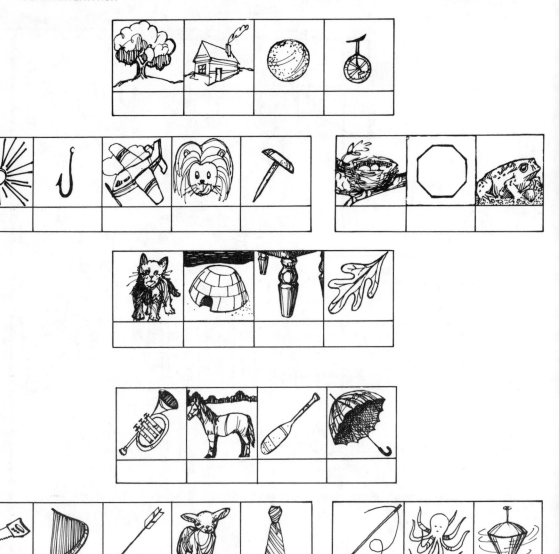

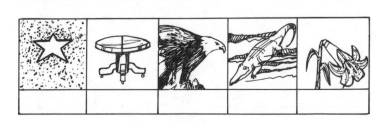

# 15. STACK-A-WORD

Put one letter in each square. The number of squares will give you a clue as to how many letters are in the word. Keep on stacking the words until you have completed the puzzle. All of the words are from the life of David, the shepherd boy who later became king of Israel.

| | |
|---|---|
| HARP | GIANT |
| BEAR | DAVID |
| LION | TEMPLE |
| KING | SOLOMON |
| SHEEP | ABSALOM |
| STONE | SHEPHERD |
| SLING | ANOINTED |
| PSALM | |

# 16. SOLOMON

Solomon is often called the wisest man who ever lived. Some of his wise sayings are written in the Old Testament book of Proverbs. Hidden in the picture on the next page are several things he talks about in Proverbs 30. Fill in the blanks below to discover what Solomon is saying. Then find those things on the next page.

v. 4    who hath gathered the wind in his _____?

v. 5    he is a _____ unto them that put their trust in him.

v. 14   whose _____ are as _____, and the jaw teeth as

_____.

v. 17   The _____ that mocketh at his father.

v. 19   the way of an _____ in the air

the way of the _____ upon a _____

the way of a _____ in the midst of the sea.

v. 25   the _____ are a people not strong.

v. 26   the _____ (often thought of as a bunny) are but a feeble folk.

v. 27   the _____ have no king.

v. 28   the _____ taketh hold with her hands.

v. 30   a _____ which is strongest among beasts.

v. 31   a _____ and a _____.

v. 32   lay thy _____ upon thy _____.

v. 33   the wringing of the _____ bringeth forth blood.

# 17. THE STORY OF RUTH

Fill in the blanks in the story, using the word list below. Then find those words hidden in the puzzle on the next page.

Because there was a famine in Bethlehem, a man named _____, his wife _____, and their two sons, _____ and _____ went to the country of _____. The family lived in Moab for some time. First the father died, and then the two sons.

The mother was sad and lonely and made plans to return to Bethlehem. Her two daughters-in-law, Orpah and _____ started to walk back with her. Naomi said, "Go back, _____ daughters."

Only Orpah turned around. Ruth went along with Naomi to Bethlehem. Ruth promised to love _____ and Naomi's people. When they got to Bethlehem, Naomi said to her friends, "Do not call me Naomi, call me _____, for the Lord hath dealt bitterly with me."

A _____ of Naomi's husband lived in Bethlehem. He was a very rich man named _____. He had many fields of corn and barley and the _____ were busy gathering the _____.

Ruth said to Naomi, "Let me now go to the _____ and _____ _____ of corn." Naomi said, "_____, my daughter."

Boaz noticed the newcomer and soon learned that she was the Moabitish girl who had come back with Naomi. He asked a close relative if he could _____ Elimelech's land. The man could not so Boaz made plans to _____ it. He took off his _____ to confirm the sale. Soon Ruth became the wife of Boaz. A little _____ was born to them and they named him _____. He was the _____ of _____.

| | | | |
|---|---|---|---|
| NAOMI | FIELD | CHILION | MAHLON |
| KINSMAN | BOAZ | REDEEM | REAPERS |
| MOAB | ELIMELECH | GLEAN | GRANDFATHER |
| DAVID | RUTH | SHOE | SON |
| GOD | BUY | MY | OBED |
| MARA | EARS | | GO |
| SHEAVES | | | |

| M | A | R | A | G | S | N | O | D |
| O | A | D | E | B | O | I | G | H |
| A | Y | H | E | I | N | D | R | T |
| B | U | G | L | E | A | N | A | U |
| O | B | I | I | O | Y | A | N | R |
| A | H | E | M | H | N | M | D | E |
| C | D | A | E | S | A | S | F | A |
| F | I | E | L | D | O | N | A | P |
| Z | V | A | E | T | M | I | T | E |
| A | A | R | C | E | I | K | H | R |
| O | D | S | H | E | A | V | E | S |
| B | O | M | E | E | D | E | R | A |

# 18. A PATIENT MAN

Job is often called a patient man. When he was suffering, he wanted to talk to God, to ask God some questions. Instead, God came to Job and asked Job some questions. Fill in the blanks below, using verses from Job 39 and then find the objects hidden in the picture.

Knowest thou the time when the wild＿＿＿＿＿＿of the rock bring forth?

They grow up with＿＿＿＿＿＿.

Who hath loosed the bands of the wild＿＿＿＿＿？

Will the＿＿＿＿＿＿be willing to serve thee?

Gavest thou the goodly wings unto the＿＿＿＿＿＿＿?

Or wings and feathers unto the ＿＿＿＿＿＿＿?

Which leaveth her＿＿＿＿＿＿in the earth?

Hast thou given the＿＿＿＿＿＿strength?

Canst thou make him afraid as a＿＿＿＿＿＿＿＿?

Doth the＿＿＿＿＿fly by thy wisdom?

Doth the＿＿＿＿＿＿mount up at thy command, and make her＿＿＿＿＿on

high?

# 19. QUEEN ESTHER'S PALACE

This is a drawing of one of the bedrooms in the palace at Shushan, the place where Queen Esther lived. The sixth verse of the first chapter of Esther says: "Where were white, green, and blue, hangings [drapes], fastened with cords of fine linen and purple to silver rings and pillars of marble; the beds were of gold and silver, upon a pavement [floor] of red, and blue, and white, and black marble." Color the picture to match the description in the Bible verse.

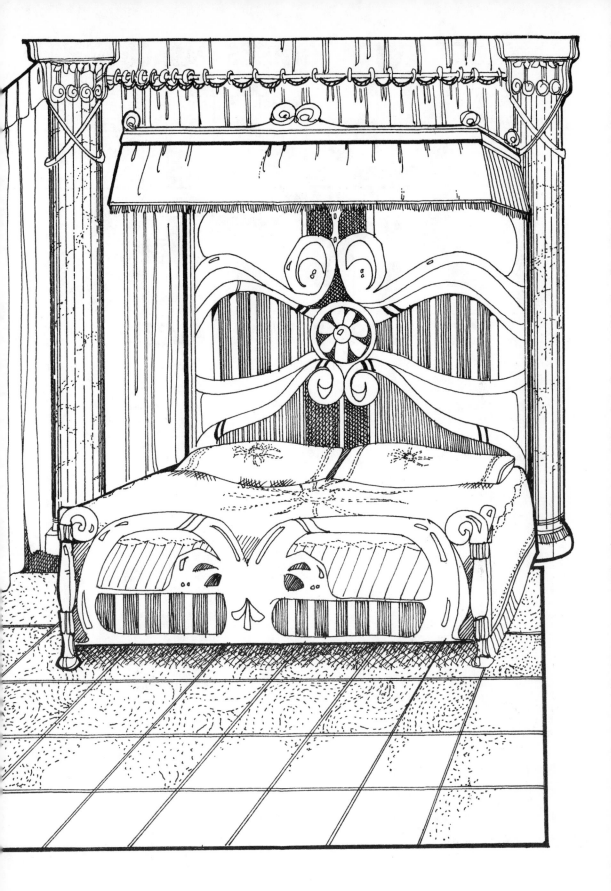

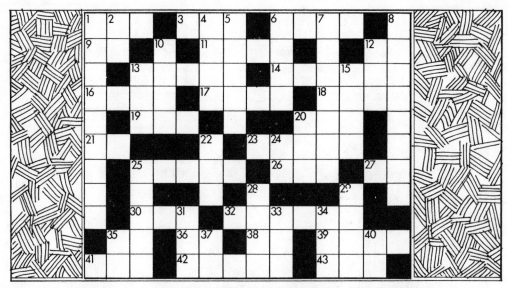

# 20. A CROSSWORD PUZZLE

Numbers 1, 3, 6, 13, 14, 25, 30, 41, 42 across are the words of a familiar text in Esther.

**ACROSS**

1 Princes from Persia ＿＿＿＿＿＿＿ Media came to Ahaseurus' feast. (Esther 1:3)
3 Second word in the Bible.
6 A man who rules.
9 ＿＿＿＿＿＿,everyone that thirsteth. Isa. 55:1
11 The first garden.
12 Depart from evil and ＿＿＿ good.
13 John was the disciple Jesus ＿＿＿＿＿＿＿＿＿.
14 Hadassah is another name for ＿＿＿＿＿＿＿＿＿.
16 Opening.
17 Eat.
18 Part of body.
19 Number following nine.
20 Person who is humorous.
21 Hebrew name for God.
23 Pigs.
25 Opposite of below.
26 What a hen lays.
27 Sixth note of musical scale.
30 Everything.
31 Ahasuerus' first wife.
35 Exact spot.
36 ＿＿＿＿ angel appeared to Zacharias.
38 Jesus went＿＿＿＿the temple.
39 Skip over.
41 Now it came to pass on＿＿＿ third day. (Esther 5:1)
42 Hegai was the keeper of the ＿＿＿＿＿＿＿. (Esther 2:8)
43 A favorite animal.

**DOWN**

1 King of 127 provinces. (Esther 1:1)
2 Opposite of yes.
4 Pay attention to.
5 Boy's nickname.
6 Joint in the leg.
7 Opposite of everything.
8 A Jew who lived in Shushan. (Esther 2:5)
10 A very tiny piece.
12 Home of a lion.
13 Abraham's nephew.
15 Opposite of love.
20 False hair worn on head.
22 First mother.
24 Us.
25 Beginning to stop.
28 A companion.
29 U.S. coin.
31 A rule.
33 Jesus is the＿＿＿＿＿＿ of God.
34 The highest part.
35 Exclamation of delight.
37 Jesus had ＿＿＿＿＿ sin.
40 For he spake and ＿＿＿＿＿was done. (Ps. 33:9)

# 21. JUGS OF OIL

There are thirty jugs of oil hidden in this picture.
How many can you find?

# 22. NEHEMIAH

Fill in the blanks, choosing words from the word list and then fit the words from the list into the Stack-a-Word puzzle on the next page.

Nehemiah lived in the palace at Shushan. He was a cupbearer for King

_____ and wanted to go back to _____ to

rebuild the city's broken _____. The city _____ were

ruined, too. They had been burned. The king gave _____

permission to return to his country.

_____, who lived near Jerusalem didn't want those

walls to be rebuilt. He joined with other _____ and _____

and tried to stop the work. In front of the army of _____, he

poked fun of the hard workers. One of the men said, "If a _____ go

up, he shall break down their stone wall. But Nehemiah and his men just went

on working on the walls and _____. They worked with one hand

while they held a _____ or a _____ in the other. Some

men held _____. One man stood guard, next to Nehemiah. He had

a _____ and was to _____ and blow it if there was

danger. All of the men were obeying Nehemiah's command to _____

and build. They knew God was with them.

Finally the wall was finished. Nehemiah counted all the people who lived

in Jerusalem. There were 42,360, not counting the servants. He counted the

animals too. There were 736 _____ besides mules and camels.

Nehemiah offered a _____ of thanksgiving. Then _____,

the scribe, brought out the Book of the Law and read the _____

to the people. They wanted to celebrate the feast of _____. The

people went out to the hills to get olive and _____, _____,

and palm branches. They promised to serve God and to bring offerings of

_____, _____, _____, and fruit. The Levites were to bring

the _____ for the offerings to the _____ or

_____. The priests were to get some of the offerings, but a part

was also for those who would _____ in the Temple.

OIL      WALLS    HORSES
FOX      TOWER    MYRTLE
CORN     GATES    VESSELS
EZRA     SPEARS   TRUMPET
PINE     BOOTHS   SAMARIA
SING     PRAYER   NEHEMIAH
WINE     SHIELD   JERUSALEM
ARISE    NOBLES   SANBALLAT
WATCH    RULERS   ARTAXERXES
SWORD    TEMPLE   ORDINANCES
                  SANCTUARY

```
S O A B O O T H S A B
Y R G N A T S W O R E
A S H I P I O M A K L
D E E P H L A P N U L
R H A S L R P P I T Y
O S R I I O D A N H R
L A B N J D N I E R C
T N E P E R I N V E S
E R Y Y T U W E E E A
S O F T J O N A H L C
E T O I A G H S I F K
M E R C I F U L D I C
R M T O L O O E V I L
O L Y A O S V E I T O
W A A T T E M P E S T
A C M T S A E S P E H
```

# 23. JONAH, THE RUNAWAY

All of these words are found in the story of Jonah, the man who tried to run away from God.

| | | | |
|---|---|---|---|
| WORM | NINEVEH | JOPPA | LOTS |
| GOURD | BELLY | MERCIFUL | THREE |
| TARSHISH | FISH | BOOTHS | LORD |
| TEMPEST | BILLOWS | PITY | EVIL |
| SHIP | FORTY | CITY | CALM |
| MARINERS | SACKCLOTH | ASHES | DIE |
| ASLEEP | REPENT | LOST | CRY |
| EAST | ANGRY | FLEE | DAYS |
| WIND | | | |

44

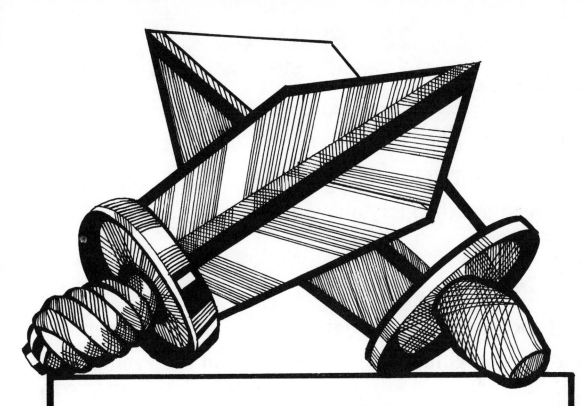

# 24. BATTLES

There are many stories of unusual battles in the Bible. See if you can fill in the blanks without looking up the references.

1. This warrior used _____, _____, and empty jars to win the battle. His name was _____. (Judges 7:15-23)

2. _____ hands were held up by _____ and _____. As long as his hands were held up, the Israelites were winning. (Exodus 17:8-14)

3. The city walls of _____ fell after the Israelites _____ around the city seven times. (Joshua 6)

4. This insect, the _____ was used to win a war with the Amorites (Joshua 24:12)

5. This battle was won because the soldiers of Syria were _____. (II Kings 6:14-23)

6. A woman named _____ won a battle by driving a _____ through the temples of a sleeping captain. (Judges 4:17-23)

# 25. PSALM 8

Color and cut out the small pictures below and, using your Bible (the King James Version), put the picture in the correct spot in the psalm.

## PSALM 8

O Lord our Lord,

how excellent is thy name in all the ☐

who hast set thy glory above the heavens.

Out of the mouth of ☐ and sucklings

hast thou ordained strength because of thine enemies,

that thou mightest still the enemy and the avenger.

When I consider thy heavens, the work of thy ☐ ,

the ☐ and the ☐ which thou hast

ordained; What is ☐ , that thou art mindful

of him?  and the son of man that thou visitest him?

For thou hast made him a little lower than the ☐,

and hast ☐ him with glory and honour.

Thou madest him to have dominion over the works

of thy ☐ ; thou hast put all things under

his ☐ : All ☐ and ☐ , and

the ☐ the field; The ☐ of the air,

and the ☐ of the sea, and whatsoever passeth
through the paths of the seas.

O   Lord our Lord,
how excellent is thy name in all the ☐

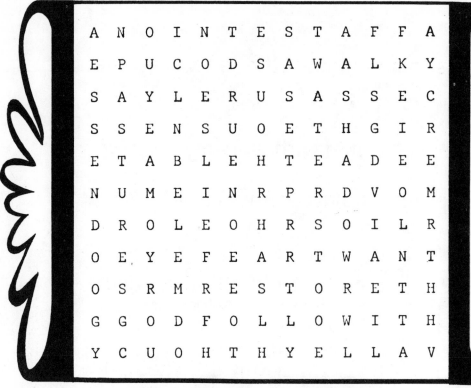

```
A N O I N T E S T A F F A
E P U C O D S A W A L K Y
S A Y L E R U S A S S E C
S S E N S U O E T H G I R
E T A B L E H T E A D E E
N U M E I N R P R D V O M
D R O L E O H R S O I L R
O E Y E F E A R T W A N T
O S R M R E S T O R E T H
G G O D F O L L O W I T H
Y C U O H T H Y E L L A V
```

# 26. FIND-A-WORD

Hidden in this puzzle are words from the Twenty-third Psalm. You may find them up, down, backward, or sideways. Not all the letters are used, but some letters are used more than once. How many words can you find without using the word list?

| | | | | |
|---|---|---|---|---|
| ART | | | | |
| THY | GOODNESS | SURELY | FEAR | ME | MERCY |
| OVER | PASTURES | FOLLOW | WITH | OIL | STAFF |
| WALK | RESTORETH | COMFORT | THOU | ROD | TABLE |
| WANT | ANOINTEST | VALLEY | GREEN | CUP | SHADOW |
| LORD | RIGHTEOUSNESS | SHEPHERD | HOUSE | LIE | WATERS |

# 27. CODED MESSAGE #1

One of the most favorite Old Testament texts is hidden in this code. See if you can break the code.

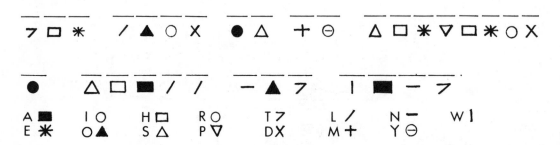

# 28.  WHO WAS AFRAID?

Many Bible people were very brave but sometimes they became very frightened too. Can you tell who these people are by looking up the text listed below the blank? Maybe you can tell by just reading the clues.

1. I was afraid to look at God and I hid my face.

   _____
   Exodus 3:6

2. A king tried to kill me with a spear but the king's son helped me escape.

   _____
   I Samuel 20

3. A wicked queen tried to kill me and I ran away. I was one of God's prophets.

   _____
   I Kings 19:3

4. A silver cup was put in my sack of grain. I was afraid the ruler would try to kill me.

   _____
   Genesis 44:12, 13

5. I deceived my brother and now he is coming to meet me. I am really scared.

   _____
   Genesis 27:27, 41

6. We ate some fruit we were not supposed to touch. God wanted to talk to us but we hid.

   _____
   Genesis 3:8-10

# 29. GOD'S WONDERFUL CARE

Psalm 91 tells about the care God takes of those who love Him. Fill in the blanks on this page and then find those objects hidden in the picture on the next page.

v. 4    He shall cover thee with his _____,

and under his _____ shalt thou trust:

his truth shall be thy _____ and buckler.

v. 5    Thou shalt not be afraid for the terror by night;

nor for the _____ that flieth by day;

v. 7    A thousand shall fall at thy side,

and ten thousand at thy right _____;

but it shall not come nigh thee.

v. 8    Only with thine _____ shalt thou behold

and see the reward of the wicked.

v. 11   For he shall give his _____ charge over thee,

to keep thee in all thy ways.

v. 12   They shall bear thee up in their hands,

lest thou dash thy _____ against a stone.

v. 13   Thou shalt tread upon the _____ and _____;

the _____ and the _____ shalt thou trample

under feet.

# 30. PSALM 104

**(17-22, 24)**

Color and cut out the small pictures below and, using your Bible (the King James Version), put the picture in the correct spot in the psalm.

Where the ____________ make their ____________:

as for the ____________, the fir ____________ are her house.

The high ____________ are a refuge for the wild ____________;

and the ____________ for the ____________.

He appointed the _____ for seasons:

the _____ knoweth his going down.

Thou maketh darkness, and it is _____:

wherein all the beasts of the forest do creep forth.

The young _____ roar after their prey,
and seek their meat from God.

The _____ ariseth, they gather themselves together,
and lay them down in their dens.

O Lord, how manifold are thy works!
in wisdom hast thou made them all:
the earth is full of thy riches.

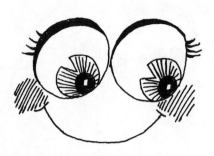

# 31.  PSALM 147

Fill in the blank words from these verses from Psalm 147 to discover which objects are hidden in the picture on the next page. Use the King James Version of the Bible.

Sing unto the Lord with thanksgiving;

sing praise upon the _____ unto our God:

Who covereth the heaven with _____,

who prepareth rain for the earth,

who maketh _____ to grow upon the _____.

He giveth to the beast his food,

and to the young _____ which cry.

He delighteth not in in the strength of the _____;

he taketh not pleasure in the _____ of a _____.

Praise the Lord, O Jerusalem;

praise thy God, O Zion.

For he hath strengthened the bars of thy _____;

he hath blessed thy _____ within thee.

He maketh peace in thy borders,

and filleth thee with the finest of the _____.

# 32. PSALM 148

Fill in the blank words from these verses from Psalm 148 to discover which objects are hidden in the picture on the next page. Use the King James Version of the Bible.

Praise ye the Lord.

Praise ye the Lord from the heavens:

praise him in the heights.

Praise ye him, all his _____;

praise ye him, all his hosts.

Praise ye him, _____ and _____;

praise him, all ye _____ of light

Praise him, ye heavens of heavens,

and ye waters that be above the heavens.

Praise the Lord from the earth,

ye _____, and all deeps;

_____, and hail; _____, and vapours;

stormy wind fulfilling his word:

_____, and all hills;

_____, and all cedars;

Beasts, and all _____;

_____, and flying _____:

_____ of the earth, and all people;

princes, and all judges of the earth:

Both _____, and maidens;

_____, and children.

Let them praise the name of the Lord:

for his name alone is excellent;

his glory is above the earth and heaven.

# 33. PSALM 150

Color and cut out the small pictures below and, using your Bible (the King James Version), put the picture in the correct spot in the psalm.

## PSALM 150

Praise ye the Lord.

Praise God in his [ ] :
praise him in the firmament of his power.

Praise him for his mighty acts:
Praise him according to his excellent greatness.

Praise him with the sound of a [ ] ;

Praise him with the [ ] and [ ] .

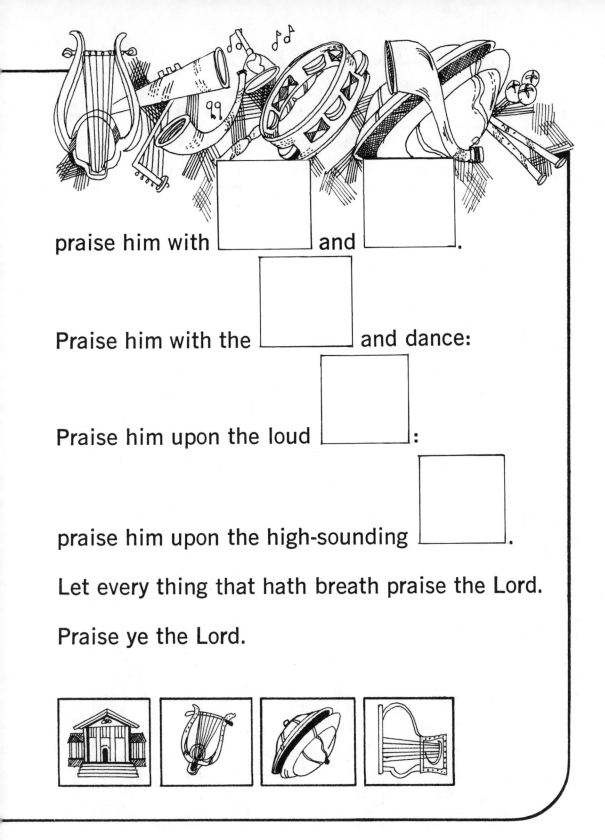

praise him with ☐ and ☐.

Praise him with the ☐ and dance:

Praise him upon the loud ☐:

praise him upon the high-sounding ☐.

Let every thing that hath breath praise the Lord.

Praise ye the Lord.

# 34. A PICTURE PROPHECY FROM ISAIAH 11

This is part of a picture Isaiah gave about the New Jerusalem. Color and cut out the pictures below and, using your Bible, (the King James Version), put the picture in the correct spot in the prophecy.

The _____ also shall dwell with the _____

and the _____ shall lie down with the _____ (young lamb)

and the _____ and the young _____ and the fatling together.

and a _____ shall lead them.

And the _____ and _____ shall feed;

their young ones shall lie down _____

and the _____ shall eat straw like the _____.

# 35. A MIGHTY GOD

Isaiah 40 tells us some wonderful things about God. Fill in the missing words below and then find the objects hidden in the picture on the next page.

v. 8    The grass withereth, the _____ fadeth; but the word of our God shall stand forever.

v. 10   Behold, the Lord God will come with a strong _____, and his his _____ shall rule for him.

v. 11   . . . he shall gather the _____ with his arm.

v. 15   Behold, the nations are as a drop of a _____.

v. 19   . . . the goldsmith . . . casteth silver _____.

v. 20   he chooseth . . . a _____ that will not rot.

v. 22   It is he that sitteth upon the _____ of the earth, and the inhabitants thereof are as _____.

v. 26   Lift up your _____ on high.

v. 31   But they that wait upon the Lord shall renew their strength; they shall mount up with _____ as _____.

# 36. A WALL OF LETTERS

To discover what is written on the bricks in this wall of letters, begin above the arrow and skip every other letter. As you pass a letter, write it on the blanks below. You must go around the wall twice to get the complete message.

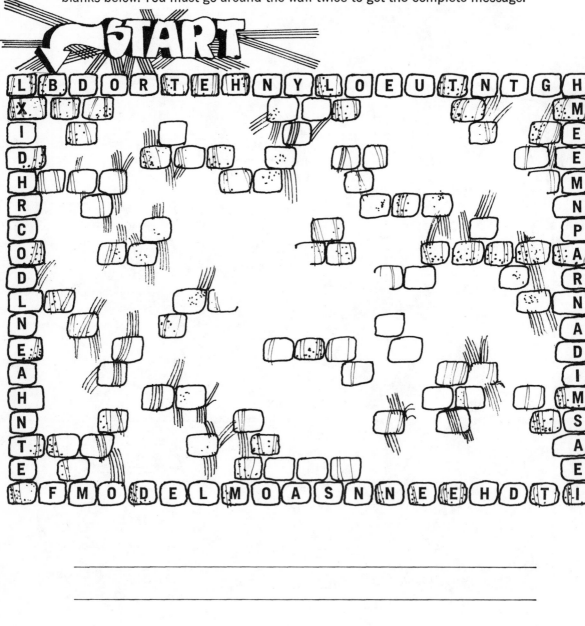

_____

_____

_____

# 37. DOT-TO-DOT

This is an animal Jeremiah talked about in chapter 13 of his book. See if you can find the verse.

# New Testament Stories

# 38. A WREATH OF LETTERS

Begin with the letter J and go around the wreath, skipping every other letter to find the hidden message. You must go around the wreath twice to use all the letters. Then color the wreath.

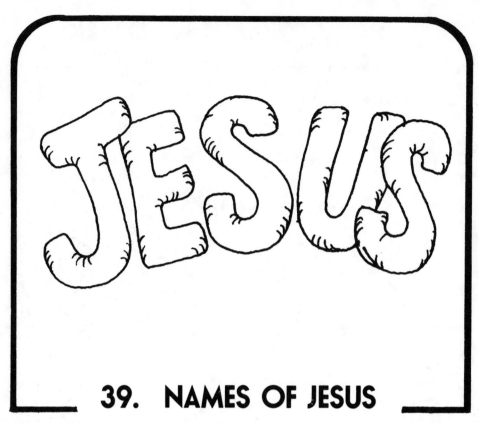

## 39. NAMES OF JESUS

Jesus is given many names in the Bible. Look up the references given below, then see if you can find the pictures of the names hidden in the picture on the next page.

Hebrews 6:19 _____

I Peter 2:8 _____

Revelation 5:5 _____

II Peter 1:19 _____

John 10:9 _____

Hosea 14:5 _____

Isaiah 4:2 _____

Jeremiah 2:13 _____

John 1:29 _____

John 9:5 _____

Isaiah 53:2 _____

# 40. A STORY JESUS TOLD

Jesus told a story about a wise man and a foolish man. Read the story in Matthew 7:24-27. Finish the dot-to-dot pictures on these pages and write below each picture whether the builder was wise or foolish.

# 41. THE "I AM'S" OF JESUS

Many times Jesus said, "I am . . ." Can you finish the I AM's below and then find them again in the picture on the next page?

I AM THE _____ John 6:35

I AM THE _____ John 9:5

I AM THE _____ John 10:7

I AM THE _____ John 10:11, 14

I AM THE _____ John 11:25

I AM THE _____ John 14:6 (3 things)

I AM THE _____ John 15:1

# 42. MAP

This is a map of Judah, Samaria, and Galilee at the time Jesus was on earth. The lines show some of the trips he made when He was young. Color the countries in yellow and orange. Color the seas blue.

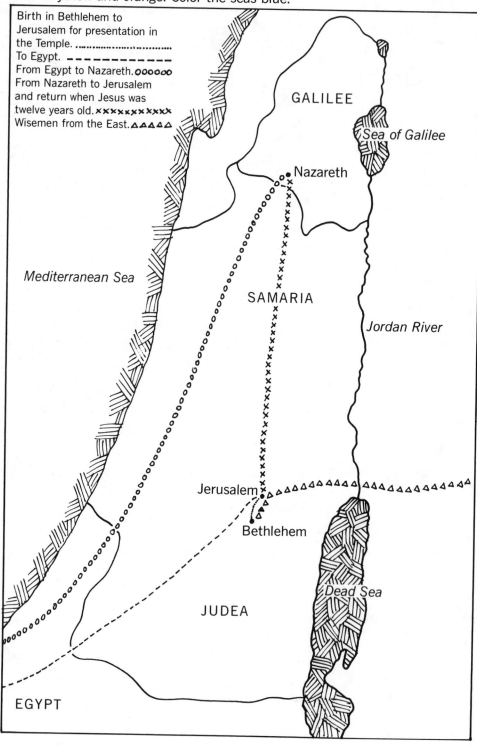

Birth in Bethlehem to Jerusalem for presentation in the Temple. ....................
To Egypt. — — — — — — —
From Egypt to Nazareth. ooooooo
From Nazareth to Jerusalem and return when Jesus was twelve years old. ×××××××××
Wisemen from the East. ▵▵▵▵▵

GALILEE

Sea of Galilee

Nazareth

Mediterranean Sea

SAMARIA

Jordan River

Jerusalem
Bethlehem

Dead Sea

JUDEA

EGYPT

|   | 1 | 2 | 3 | 4 | 5 | 6 | 7 | 8 | 9 | 10 | 11 |
|---|---|---|---|---|---|---|---|---|---|----|----|
| ➤ | W | I | H | C | O | O | S | N | O | F | E |
|   | V | E | E | S | R | S | T | A | H | L | E |
|   | R | S | E | O | F | B | O | E | R | F | E |
|   | S | O | H | R | A | E | L | M | L | Y | C |
|   | O | F | N | A | F | T | E | H | S | E | S |
|   | M | R | E | W | B | H | E | I | F | C | O |
|   | R | H | E | I | M | S | E | I | N | N | H |
|   | I | H | M | E | W | A | I | V | L | E | L | N |

## 43.  A WALL OF LETTERS

To unscramble the message in this wall of letters, use only the letters in the
odd-numbered columns the first time through. On the second try, use only
the letters in the even-numbered squares. Write the message on the lines
below the wall.

_____ _____ \_\_\_\_\_ _____
\_\_ _____ \_\_\_, \_\_\_ \_\_\_\_ \_ _____
\_\_\_\_ _____ \_\_ _____ \_\_\_\_\_ \_\_ \_\_ \_\_\_\_\_.

# 44. MATTHEW, THE TAX COLLECTOR

How many wrong things can you find in this picture?

# 45. THE LOST COIN

Jesus told the story of the woman who lost a coin (Luke 15:8-10). She swept the house until she found it. Can you help her spot it?

# 46. GOD'S WORD

Skip every other letter in two trips around the circle. Print the letters on the blanks inside the circle.

# 47. A PROMISE FROM JESUS

Hidden in the spaces marked with a dot is a promise from Jesus. Color these spaces red. Fill in the spaces marked with an X using your favorite color.

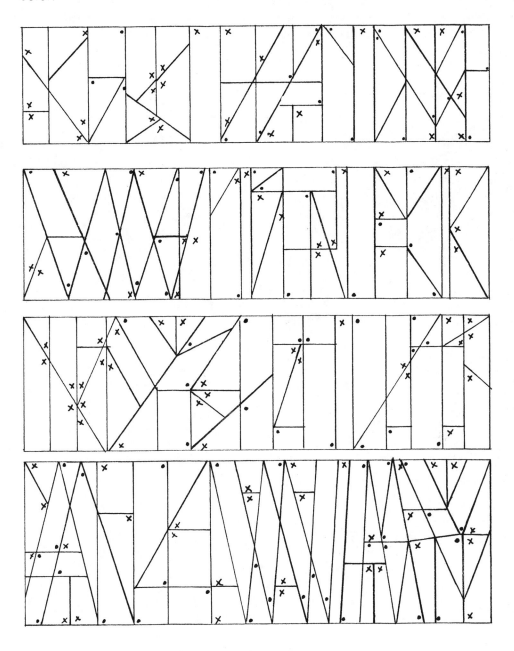

81

# 48. THREE DISCIPLES

Jesus had twelve disciples but three were His favorites. You can make a triangle with a picture of the disciples if you follow these directions carefully.

First color the pictures. You may also want to color the background, using a different background for each section. Then cut out on the solid lines. Fold along the dotted lines. Tape the tabs together with masking tape or scotch tape.

# 49.  THE LOST SHEEP

Remember the story Jesus told about the one lost sheep? Read about it in Luke 15:3-7. While this shepherd took a nap, twelve of his sheep disappeared. Can you help him find them?

# 50. TWELVE BASKETS

After Jesus fed the 5,000 people, His disciples picked up twelve baskets of leftovers. Can you find all twelve baskets hidden in this picture?

# 51. THE LOST COINS

Jesus told a story about a lady who lost one coin. Read it in Luke 15:8-10. This lady lost twenty-four coins. Can you help her find them?

# 52. FOLLOWERS OF JESUS

There are some rules that all of those who love Jesus obey. Look up the references to fill in the missing words. Then color in the first letter of the missing word each time the letter appears in the puzzle below. If you follow the color code exactly, the first letter of what followers of Jesus are called will appear.

Be ye ☐ __ __ __ one to another. Ephesians 4:32 (Use blue for this letter)

☐ __ __ __ one another. I John 4:7 (Use yellow for this letter)

Do that which is ☐ __ __ __ __. II Corinthians 13:7 (Use green for this letter)

☐ __ __ __ __ for one another. James 5:16 (Use red for this letter)

```
        B K G O
      T U T A D M
    Y B O D Y G O E
    D O N S T U T A M E
  A A D J V G E A S O T A
  Y B T S E M O H Q S Q Y
  I E R L K K P K K L O T
  Y O R L P R L R L K P K J M
  I S L R K L P K P L R L A I
  E I K P H O T E A R L P E T
  E A R K L E S U I L P R A T
  I S P P K I H E H S T A U B
  T A L K R O H F A B H I C I
  I T R P K H E A D I N G B O
  I S L K L D M I N D E H F O
  T O P P R O T T E H I N G O
  D N R L K I N G T L P R E A
  I E R K R P H P K P K R E A
  O K L P R L R L K P L O
  H S R L K K P K K R E T
  O O A I E I A O B D
  E E I N E O O I A A
  G D G N N T S I
  N G A T E D
  T A S N
```

# 53. CODED MESSAGE #2

What good rule did Jesus give us?

‾‾  ‾‾
21 11  2 19  2  9  4 19  2      1 14 14     21 11  3 16 10 20

‾‾  ‾‾  ‾‾  ‾‾  ‾‾
23 11  1 21 20  4  2 22  2 19    24  2    23  4  5 14  8    21 11  1 21

‾‾      ‾‾      ‾‾      ‾‾  ‾‾,
15  2 16     20 11  4  5 14  8      8  4     21  4     24  4  5

‾‾      ‾‾      ‾‾      ‾‾      ‾‾  ‾‾:
 8  4     24  2     2 22  2 16    20  4    21  4    21 11  2 15

‾‾      ‾‾      ‾‾      ‾‾      ‾‾      ‾‾
 9  4 19    21 11  3 20    3 20    21 11  2    14  1 23    1 16  8

‾‾      ‾‾  ‾‾.      ‾‾      7:12
21 11  2    17 19  4 17 11  2 21 20     15  1 21 21 11  2 23

**The Key:**

| 1 | 2 | 3 | 4 | 5 | 6 | 7 | 8 | 9 | 10 | 11 | 12 | 13 | 14 | 15 | 16 | 17 | 18 | 19 | 20 | 21 | 22 | 23 | 24 |
|---|---|---|---|---|---|---|---|---|----|----|----|----|----|----|----|----|----|----|----|----|----|----|----|
| A | E | I | O | U | B | C | D | F | G  | H  | J  | K  | L  | M  | N  | P  | Q  | R  | S  | T  | V  | W  | Y  |

# 54. JESUS SAID

Fit one letter in each column into a square above the column. A colored square means the end of a word. When you have solved the puzzle, read across the squares to discover what Jesus said. The first puzzle is easy. The last one is the hardest.

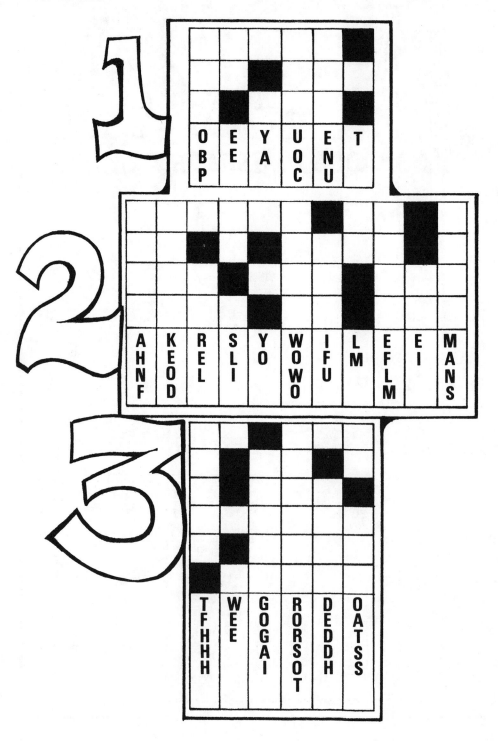

89

# 55. THE TWELVE DISCIPLES

Jesus chose twelve men to help Him while He was here on earth. These men were called disciples or apostles. Just before He left to go to heaven, Jesus told the disciples to go all over the world to preach the gospel.

In the first puzzle the names of the disciples are listed but a part of each letter is missing. Fill in the broken part of each letter.

| | |
|---|---|
| 1 ANDREW | 7 MATTHEW |
| 2 SIMON PETER | 8 THOMAS |
| 3 JAMES | 9 BARTHOLOMEW |
| 4 JOHN | |
| 5 JUDE | 10 SIMON THE ZEALOT |
| 6 NATHANIEL | 11 JUDE |
| | 12 JUDAS ISCARIOT |

Here are the names of the twelve disciples again but this time the letters are scrambled.

1  SHOMAT   _____

2  SINMO HET AZELOT   _____

3  WAREND   _____

4  HOJN   _____

5  MEAJS   _____

6  DUSAJ ROICASIT   _____

7  PIPHIL   _____

8  SADUJ   _____

9  WHATTME   _____

10  NISMO TREEP   _____

11  SEAMJ THE NSO FO LAPHAUSE   _____

12  LANANATHE   _____

God said this about Himself.

| | | | | | | | |
|---|---|---|---|---|---|---|---|
| — | — — | — — —, | — — — | — — — — — | — — | — — — — |
| 3 | 1 17 | 12 4 10 | 1 18 10 | 23 13 2 21 2 | 3 22 | 18 4 18 2 |

| | | | | | |
|---|---|---|---|---|---|
| — — — —; | — | — — | — — —, | — — — — — | — — |
| 2 16 22 2 | 3 | 1 17 | 12 4 10 | 1 18 10 | 23 13 2 21 2 | 3 22 |

| | | | |
|---|---|---|---|
| — — — — | — — — — | — —, | — — — — — — — — | — — — |
| 18 4 18 2 | 16 3 15 2 | 17 2 | 10 2 9 16 1 21 3 18 12 | 23 13 2 |

| | | | |
|---|---|---|---|
| — — — | — — — — | — — — | — — — — — — — —, |
| 2 18 10 | 11 21 4 17 | 23 13 2 | 8 2 12 3 18 18 3 18 12 |

| | | |
|---|---|---|
| — — — | — — — — | — — — — — — | — — — — |
| 1 18 10 | 11 21 4 17 | 1 18 9 3 2 18 23 | 23 3 17 2 22 |

| | | | | |
|---|---|---|---|---|
| — — — | — — — — — — | — — — — | — — — | — — — |
| 23 13 2 | 23 13 3 18 12 22 | 23 13 1 23 | 1 21 2 | 18 4 23 |

| | | |
|---|---|---|
| — — — | — — — —. | — — — — — — |
| 25 2 23 | 10 4 18 2 | 3 22 1 3 1 13 |

46:9, 10

The Key:

| 1 | 2 | 3 | 4 | 5 | 6 | 7 | 8 | 9 | 10 | 11 | 12 | 13 | 14 | 15 | 16 | 17 | 18 | 19 | 20 | 21 | 22 | 23 | 24 | 25 |
|---|---|---|---|---|---|---|---|---|---|---|---|---|---|---|---|---|---|---|---|---|---|---|---|---|
| A | E | I | O | U | Y | W | B | C | D | F | G | H | J | K | L | M | N | P | Q | R | S | T | V | Y |

# 57. JOHN, THE DISCIPLE JESUS LOVED

In this story about John some words are missing. Fill in the missing words and then find the words hidden in the puzzle on the next page.

John's father was a fisherman named _____ (Mark 1:19, 20). John and his brother James were called by Jesus to _____ Him. Because the brothers had such quick tempers, Jesus called them "Boanerges" or "_____ of _____ " (Mark 3:17). When some Samaritan people rejected Jesus, _____ and James wanted to call down _____ from _____ (Luke 9:52-56). Their mother asked Jesus to let her sons sit one on his right _____ and the other on his _____ when He came into His kingdom (Matt. 20:20-22). She didn't understand what kind of _____ Jesus was.

John loved Jesus and often Jesus chose John to go with Him. One time John saw Jesus raise the daughter of _____ (Mark 5:37) from the _____ (Mark 5:22-23, 37). He was also with Jesus on the mountain when Jesus was _____ _____ (Matt. 17:1-2).

At the Last _____ John sat next to Jesus (John 13:23). When Jesus was on the cross, He _____ John to take care of _____, Christ's _____ (John 19:25-27). John was one of the first _____ to see the empty _____ (John 20:1-10). That same day he saw the _____ Christ (John 20:19-30).

After Pentecost, John worked closely with _____ to spread the Good News (Acts 3:1). Both were sent to _____ to continue the work begun by _____ (Acts 8:5, 14).

John wrote five New Testament books: The Gospel of John, The _____ Epistle of John, The Second _____ of John, The Third Epistle of John, and the last book in the Bible, _____ . Probably the best known text in the Bible is found in John's Gospel, chapter _____, verse _____.

# 58. FIND-A-WORD

```
R A I R A M A S U R I A J E
E K I N G P T S R I F A O S
D E R U G I F S N A R T H S
N O I B E L E O T J E O N E
U Z S O R I L C L A H M E L
H S E O I H O E T L T B V P
T A N B F P E T E R O S A I
G S N O E B S N O S M W E C
I K O D E D A E E R H T H S
R E P P U S E P I S T L E I
A D E A D N E E T X I S O D
R E V E L A T I O N Y R A M
```

# 59. A MESSAGE FROM JOHN'S LETTER

In his Epistles (letters) John often used the words, "My little children." He isn't writing only to little children but to Christians of all ages when he gives the message below.

To find out what John is saying, put the letters in the columns into the squares, one letter to a square. A black square means the end of a word. The first word has seven letters and begins with the letter B.

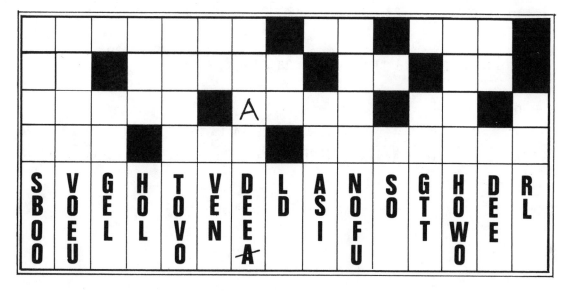

What answer did Jesus give to the lawyer who asked Him which commandment was the most important?

14 2 22 5 22    22 1 3 10    5 18 23 4    13 3 17,    23 13 4 5

22 13 1 16 23    16 4 24 2    23 13 2    16 4 21 10    23 13 6

12 4 10    7 3 23 13    1 16 16    23 13 6    13 2 1 21 23,

1 18 10    7 3 23 13    1 16 16    23 13 6    22 4 5 16,    1 18 10

7 3 23 13    1 16 16    23 13 6    17 3 18 10.    23 13 3 22

3 22    23 13 2    11 3 21 22 23    1 18 10    12 21 2 1 23

9 4 17 17 1 18 10 17 2 18 23.    1 18 10    23 13 2    22 2 9 4 18 10

3 22    16 3 15 2    5 18 23 4    3 23,    23 13 4 5    22 13 1 16 23

16 4 24 2    23 13 6    18 2 3 12 13 8 4 5 21    1 22

23 13 6 22 2 16 11.    17 1 23 23 13 2 7    22: 37–39

The Key:

| 1 | 2 | 3 | 4 | 5 | 6 | 7 | 8 | 9 | 10 | 11 | 12 | 13 | 14 | 15 | 16 | 17 | 18 | 19 | 20 | 21 | 22 | 23 | 24 |
|---|---|---|---|---|---|---|---|---|----|----|----|----|----|----|----|----|----|----|----|----|----|----|----|
| A | E | I | O | U | Y | W | B | C | D | F | G | H | J | K | L | M | N | P | Q | R | S | T | V |

# 61. STEPPINGSTONES

Who climbed a tree so that he could get a good look at Jesus? Begin at the top arrow and go to the bottom arrow in eight moves to get the right answer.

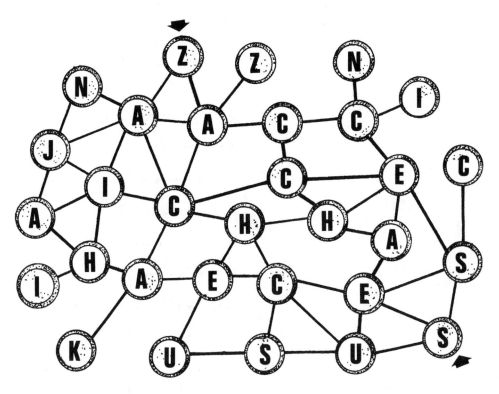

Now step over these stones in eight moves to spell out the name of the city where Jesus was born. Watch out! this one is tricky.

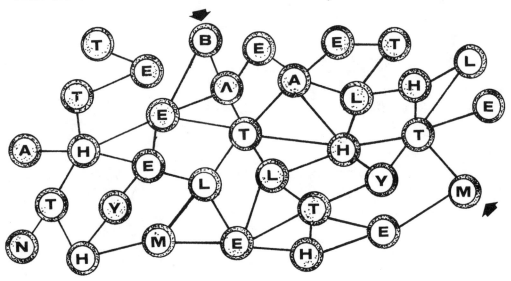

# 62. MONEY IN THE MOUTH

In Matthew 17:24-27 is the story of a fish with money in its mouth. That was one of the miracles Jesus performed.

Take ten steps down this ladder to change the word FISH to COIN. Change one letter at a time. Use the definitions at the side to help you. Then finish the picture and color it.

1. Plate, used when eating.
2. A round circle.
3. A piece of furniture.
4. Just before night.
5. Very fine dirt.
6. Old English way of saying, "Do."
7. Price.
8. Piece of clothing.
9. Black, solid, used for heat.
10. Many circles, attached.

FISH

| | |
|---|---|
| 1 | |
| 2 | |
| 3 | |
| 4 | |
| 5 | |
| 6 | |
| 7 | |
| 8 | |
| 9 | |
| 10 | |

COIN

# 63. JESUS USED IT

Jesus used this for both a bed and a pulpit. What would you use it for?

# 64. WHAT'S FOR LUNCH?

Read the story of the boy who gave his lunch away that's found in John 6. Then make a picture of that lunch by coloring the Y spaces yellow and the B spaces brown. You may color the leftover spaces with your favorite color.

# 65. PETER'S DENIAL

Jesus told Peter, ". . . that this night, before the _____ crow, thou shalt deny me thrice." Follow the dots to see a picture of the word that goes in the blank.

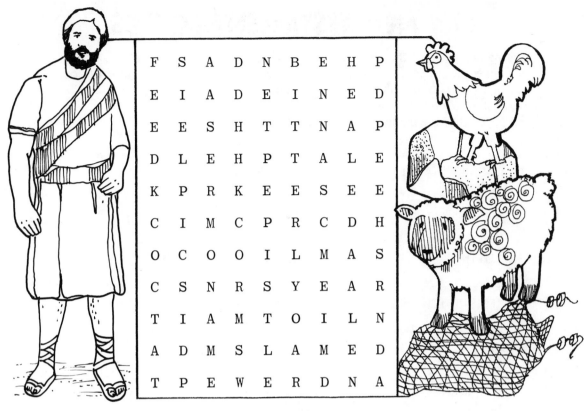

| | | | | | | | | |
|---|---|---|---|---|---|---|---|---|
| F | S | A | D | N | B | E | H | P |
| E | I | A | D | E | I | N | E | D |
| E | E | S | H | T | T | N | A | P |
| D | L | E | H | P | T | A | L | E |
| K | P | R | K | E | E | S | E | E |
| C | I | M | C | P | R | C | D | H |
| O | C | O | O | I | L | M | A | S |
| C | S | N | R | S | Y | E | A | R |
| T | I | A | M | T | O | I | L | N |
| A | D | M | S | L | A | M | E | D |
| T | P | E | W | E | R | D | N | A |

# 66. PETER

Peter was one of Jesus' disciples. Hidden in the puzzle are several words that tell about Peter and his life.

CEPHAS
ROCK
ANDREW
DISCIPLE
FISHERMAN
NET

EPISTLE
SERMON
HEALED
LAME
MAN
PENTECOST

DENIED
COCK
WEPT
BITTERLY
FEED
SHEEP

What did Peter say about Jesus?

DAN EW EEELIVB NDA EAR EURS TTHA OHTU TAR HATT RISTHC, ETH ONS

_____

FO ETH GIILNV ODG. NOJH 6:69

_____

# 67. NEW TESTAMENT BOOKS

The names of all of the New Testament books are listed below but the letters are mixed up. Unscramble the letters and put the books in the right order on the blanks. Then find all the names of the books hidden in the picture on the next page. (Note: if there is more than one book with the same name, like Peter or John, the name is hidden only once in the picture.)

1. DOCNES STANNEALSHOIS

    _____

2. MESJA

    _____

3. SUTTI

    _____

4. TFRIS IIOTCNNHRAS

    _____

5. KULE

    _____

6. MNRSOA

    _____

7. DECSON MTYIHOT

    _____

8. EHT STCA

    _____

9. SOONLICASS

    _____

10. CDEONS OHJN

    _____

11. TINSAAALG

    _____

12. STRIF ETPER

    _____

13. PIIAIPLPHSN

    _____

14. EREBSHW

    _____

15. AETHWMT

    _____

16. ILANEVETOR

    _____

17. NEDSOC TIOHCANNISR

    _____

18. RKAM

    _____

19. HIDRT JHNO

    _____

20. TFRIS LOANSSHINESTA

    _____

21. UJED

    _____

22. STIFR MTYIHOT

    _____

23. LINEMHOP

    _____

24. NJHO

    _____

25. PHINSSAEE

    _____

26. RSTIF ONHJ

    _____

27. CODNES REETP

    _____

103

# 68. CODED MESSAGE #5

What advice did the Apostle Paul give to young Timothy?

```
—  — —        — — — — ,     —     — — —       — —     — — —,
6  5 21      21 11  4  5      4     15  1 16     4 9     10 4  8

—  — — —      — — — — —      — — — — — —;      — — —
9 14  2  2    21 11  2 20 2   21 11  3 16 10 20   1 16  8

— — — — — —      — — — —      — — — — — — — — —.
9  4 14 14  4 23    1  9 21  2 19   19  3 10 11 21  2  4  5 20

— — — —,      — — — — — — — — —,      — — — — —,
16  2 20 20    10  4  8 14  3 16  2 20 20    9  1  3 21 11

— — — —,      — — — — — — — —,      — — — — — — —.
14  4 22  2    17  1 21  3  2 16  7  2    15  2  2 13 16  2 20 20

— — — — —      — — —      — — —      — — — — —
9  3 10 11 21   21 11  2   10  4  4  8   9  3 10 11 21

— —      — — — — —,      — — —      — — — —      — —
4  9      9  1  3 21 11    14  1 24    11  4 14  8    4 16

— — — — — —      — — — —.
2 21  2 19 16  1 14    14  3  9  2

                              — — — — —      — — — — — —      6:11—12.
                              9  3 19 20 21    21  3 15  4 21 11 24
```

## The Key:

| 1 | 2 | 3 | 4 | 5 | 6 | 7 | 8 | 9 | 10 | 11 | 12 | 13 | 14 | 15 | 16 | 17 | 18 | 19 | 20 | 21 | 22 | 23 | 24 |
|---|---|---|---|---|---|---|---|---|----|----|----|----|----|----|----|----|----|----|----|----|----|----|----|
| A | E | I | O | U | B | C | D | F | G | H | J | K | L | M | N | P | Q | R | S | T | V | W | Y |

# Miscellaneous

# 69. BIBLE QUESTIONS

Can you complete the following questions without looking up the reference?

1. If God be for us _____?
   Romans 8:31

2. Can the leopard _____?
   Jeremiah 13:23

3. Who made man's _____?
   Exodus 4:11

4. Could not thou watch _____?
   Mark 14:37

5. Am I my brother's _____?
   Genesis 4:9

6. Why do you call me "Lord, Lord" and _____?
   Luke 6:46

7. Judas, would you _____?
   Luke 22:48

8. Where is your _____?
   Luke 8:25

9. Who _____ me?
   Luke 8:45

10. How shall they hear _____?
    Romans 10:14

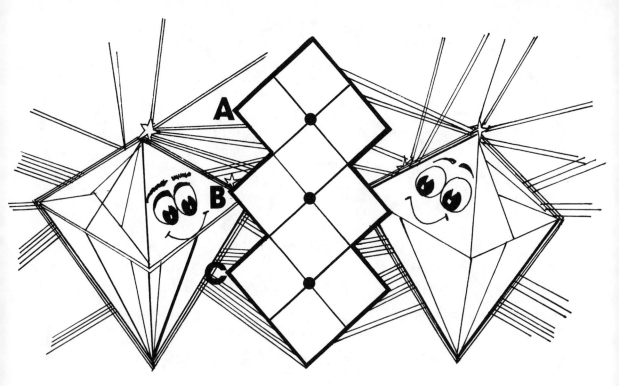

# 70. DIGIT DIAMONDS

Arrange the numbers in the squares so that the squares surrounding each circle will total twenty. Here are some clues to help you.

Section A

_____ Number of commandments given to Moses on Mt. Sinai.

_____ How many fish did Jesus use to feed the 5,000? (Matthew 14:17)

_____ How many stones did David use to kill Goliath? (I Samuel 17:49)

_____ How many times hotter did Nebuchadnezzar command the furnace to be heated for Daniel and his three friends?

Section B

_____ How many of the books of the New Testament have only one chapter?

_____ How many lepers did not return to thank Jesus for healing?

_____ How many waterpots did Jesus use on his first miracle? (John 2:6)

Section C

_____ How many people were in the ark with Noah during the flood (include Noah in the count).

_____ How many of the ten virgins did not take extra oil? (Matthew 25:3)

_____ The number of days Jesus was in the grave.

# 71. TWO MESSAGES

The first message is from the prophet Jeremiah. To find out what he said, put one letter from the columns below into each square. A black square means the end of a word.

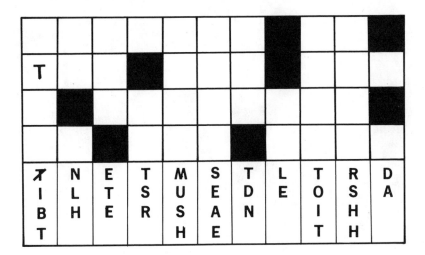

The second message is one from Jesus himself. To find out what it is, put one letter from the columns into each square. A black square means the end of a word.

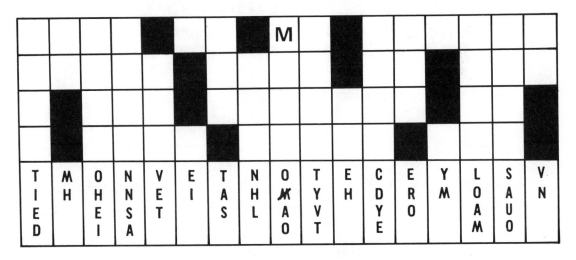

# 72. LITTLE THINGS

The Bible talks about many little things that are important. Unscramble the words below and fill in the correct blanks. Use the Bible references to check your answers.

1. David chose five smooth _____    I Samuel 17:40

2. _____ in thy brother's eye    Matthew 7:3

3. the widow put in two _____    Luke 21:2

4. _____ of your head are numbered    Luke 12:7

5. faith as a grain of _____ _____    Matthew 17:20

6. the _____ is a little member (of the body)    James 3:5

|              |                 |
|--------------|-----------------|
| TOME         | SHARI           |
| TIMES        | TENSOS          |
| GETUNO       | RATSMUD DESE    |

# 73. GOD SAID THIS

God gave a special promise in one of the psalms. Cross out every third letter to unscramble the message.

HEMSHOALTLCDALELURPOTNMAE,

ANTDINWIOLLEANTSWOERDHILM:

IWWILTLBEEWHITOHHEIMEINOTRIOUTBLUE;

IWBILTLDOELAIVEERTHISM,

ANGDHPONKORDHIPM.

# 74. GOOD ADVICE

# 75.  GOLDEN OBJECTS

The Bible talks about many things made of gold. Look up the references given below and write down the name of the golden object. Then look for it hidden in the drawing on the next page.

1.  Psalm 21:3          _____

2.  Exodus 32:3         _____

3.  Ecclesiastes 12:6   _____

4.  Revelation 17:4     _____

5.  Exodus 25:26        _____

6.  Esther 1:6          _____

7.  Proverbs 25:11      _____

8.  Psalm 68:13         _____

9.  Exodus 28:34        _____

10.  Numbers 7:26       _____

11.  I Samuel 6:4       _____

12.  Esther 5:2         _____

13.  Revelation 1:12    _____

14.  Genesis 41:42      _____

15.  Exodus 25:38       _____

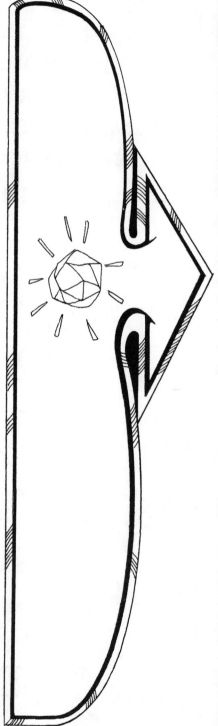

# 76. BIBLE BEEHIVE

All of these Bible verses have a "be" in them. Some of the other words have been left out too. How many texts can you complete without looking up the Bible reference?

1. And_____ye_____ one to another. Eph. 4:32

2. _____ye therefore _____ of _____ as dear children. Eph. 5:1

3. _____ _____ in the Lord. Eph.6:10

4. Commit thy works unto the_____, and thy_____shall

_____ _____. Prov. 16:3

5. And_____ye _____. Col. 3:15

6. That ye_____ to _____ _____. I Thess. 4:11

7. _____thou an _____ of the believers in word, in conversation.
I Tim. 4:12

8. _____not_____ in thine own_____; fear the_____,

and_____from evil. Prov. 3:7

9. _____ _____ for nothing; but in every thing by prayer and sup-

plication with thanksgiving let your requests_____ _____ _____

unto God. Phil. 4:6

10. Ask, and it shall_____ _____ you; seek, and ye shall find; knock, and

it shall_____ _____ unto you. Matt. 7:7

11. For where your_____is, there will your _____ _____

also. Matt. 6:21

# 77. WHERE DID THEY LIVE?

Not all Bible people lived in houses. Match these people with the place they lived.

| | |
|---|---|
| Lot | temple |
| Noah | among tombstones |
| Man with unclean spirits | palace |
| Moses | garden |
| Adam and Eve | tent |
| John the Baptist | outside a rich man's gate |
| Lazarus | desert |
| Samuel | large boat |

# 78. RIDES

People rode on animals and other things in Bible times. Match these riders with the vehicle they used.

| | |
|---|---|
| Abraham's servant | bed |
| Balaam | horses and chariots |
| Jesus | camel |
| Elijah | basket and rope |
| Paul | ass |
| Noah | colt |
| Moses | fiery chariot |
| The paralytic | ark |
| Pharoah's army | basket of bulrushes |

# 79. WHAT DID THEY EAT?

Sometimes Bible people ate unusual things. Match the person with the thing he or she ate.

| | |
|---|---|
| John the Baptist | manna |
| Esau | locusts |
| Eve | kernels of corn |
| The disciples | fruit |
| David | pottage |
| The Israelites | showbread |

# 80. I-A-H NAMES

Several men mentioned in the Bible had names that ended with the same last three letters — I-A-H. How many can you identify without looking up the Bible verse?

1. I had charge of rebuilding the wall and Temple at Jerusalem. (Ezra 2:2) _____ IAH

2. I was a king of Judah, the son of Ahab. I ruled for only 2 years. (I Kings 22:40) _____ IAH

3. I, too, was a king of Judah, the son of Joash. I ruled for 23 years. (II Kings 14:1) _____ IAH

4. I was the Old Testament prophet who said, "Here am I, send me." _____ IAH

5. I was a king of Judah who loved God. God added 15 years to my life when I prayed for healing. (II Kings 20:1-11) _____ IAH

6. I was only 16 years old when I was made king of Judah. (II Kings 15:1-2) _____ IAH

7. Nebuchadnezzar made me a vassal-king of Judah. (II Kings 24:17) _____ IAH

8. People call me "the weeping prophet." _____ IAH

9. I prophesied in Judah and am known as the fourth Minor Prophet. _____ IAH

10. I wrote an Old Testament book that has 8 visions and am known as the eleventh Minor Prophet. _____ IAH

11. I was only 8 years old when I became king. (II Kings 22:1, 2) _____ IAH

12. I was a royal prince. The prophet Jeremiah was thrown in my dungeon. (Jer. 21:1) _____ IAH

If you're ready for some more puzzlers, these names all end in E - L. Most of them are easy to guess. Scripture references are found with the less familiar names.

1. I grew up in the temple. _____ EL

2. My mother and I were chased into the desert. _____ EL

3. I taught Paul. He was a good student. (Acts 22:3) _____ EL

4. I am the father of Laban. (Gen. 25:20) _____ EL

5. I carved wood, set in precious stones, did some of the gold, silver, and copper work for the Tabernacle. (Exod. 31:1-11) _____ EL

6. My 3 friends were thrown into the fiery furnace. _____ EL

# 81.
# COUNTING SHEEP

The shepherd wants to get all the sheep into the sheepfold before night comes. Draw a circle around the number of sheep that matches the answer to each question. If you answer correctly, your total will be thirty-six and all the sheep will get into the fold.

_____ 1. Number of creation days

_____ 2. Number of Jesus' disciples

_____ 3. Number of loaves the little boy had

_____ 4. Number of wise virgins

_____ 5. Number of fishes the little boy had

_____ 6. Number of days Jesus was in the tomb

_____ 7. Number of crosses on Calvary

# 82. LET'S GO FISHING

Brett loves to fish. Help him catch all the fish swimming around in the pool. Draw a circle around the number of fish that matches the answer to the question. Brett knows that the answer to the first question is one and he has already put a circle around one fish. Now it's your turn. If you answer all the questions correctly, all the fish should be inside circles.

1. How many windows were in Noah's ark? (Gen. 6:16) _____

2. How many fish did Jesus use when He fed 5,000 people? (John 6:9) _____

3. How many tables of stone did Moses use when he wrote the Ten Commandments? (Exod. 34:28-29) _____

4. How many people were saved inside Noah's ark? (Gen. 7:13) _____

5. How many fingers on each hand and how many toes on each foot did one of the sons of a giant have? (I Chron. 20:6) _____

6. How many books in the Bible are named after women? _____

7. How many stones did David pick up when he went out to kill the giant? (I Sam. 17:40) _____

8. How many children did Abraham and Sarah have? (Gen. 21:3) _____

9. How many sons did Isaac and Rebekah have? (Gen. 25:24) _____

10. How many disciples did Jesus take with Him when He went to the Mount of Transfiguration? (Matt. 17:1) _____

# 83. MORDECAI'S MESSAGE

Mordecai had a special message for his niece, Esther. To find out what he said, put the letters in the columns into the squares. A black square means the end of a word.

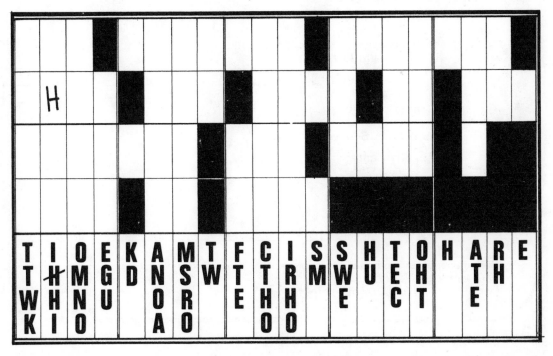

# 84.
# WHO AM I?

Give yourself 5 points if you can guess the name of the Bible person described by the first clue. You rate only 3 points if you need 2 clues, and 1 point if you need 3 clues.

1. I am a fisherman.
   My brother's name is Andrew.
   I denied Christ three times.

   My name is _____ Points: _____

2. I am the first king of Israel.
   My son's name is Jonathan.
   I was jealous of David.

   My name is _____ Points: _____

3. I am a woman of Moab.
   I learned to love Israel's God.
   My husband's name is Boaz.

   My name is _____ Points: _____

4. I am a very large Philistine.
   All of the Israelite soldiers were afraid of me.
   I fought with David and lost.

   My name is _____ Points: _____

5. The angel Gabriel came to see me.
   I had a special baby.
   My baby was born in Bethlehem.

   My name is _____ Points: _____

6. I am the Light of the World.
   I am the Bread of Life.
   I am the Son of God.

   My name is _____ Points: _____

7. Both my mother and grandmother were Christians.
   Paul wrote two letters to me.
   I am one of Paul's favorite helpers.

   My name is _____ Points: _____

8. My father gave me a beautiful coat.
   I have some very jealous brothers.
   I am a very important ruler in Egypt.

   My name is _____ Points: _____

# 85. ANOTHER WHO AM I?

Give yourself 5 points if you can guess the name of the Bible person described by the first clue. You rate only 3 points if you need 2 clues and 1 point if you need 3 clues.

1.  I bought some very expensive perfume.
    I poured the perfume over Jesus.
    I wiped Jesus' feet with my hair.

    My name is _____ Points _____

2.  I had very long, beautiful hair.
    I was the son of a famous king of Israel.
    My hair caught in the bough of a tree.

    My name is _____ Points _____

3.  When I was hungry, birds brought me food.
    Once I called fire down from heaven.
    I went to heaven without dying.

    My name is _____ Points _____

4.  Before I was born, God planned that I would be a prophet.
    God told me to wear a wooden yoke around my neck.
    I was called the "Weeping Prophet."

    My name is _____ Points _____

5.  I am not an Israelite.
    I am a general.
    I was cured of leprosy.

    My name is _____ Points _____

6.  I am a tax collector.
    I am one of Jesus' disciples.
    I wrote the first book in the New Testament.

    My name is _____ Points _____

7.  A crowd came to my door early in the morning.
    I washed my hands in front of the crowd.
    I couldn't find any fault in Jesus.

    My name is _____ Points _____

8.  Paul called me his son.
    I had work to do in Crete.
    One of the New Testament books was written to me.

    My name is _____ Points _____

# 86. MEN IN THE BIBLE

Hidden in these pictures are the letters in the names of some men in the Bible. One clue is under each picture. How many names can you unscramble without looking at the answers?

1. One of Paul's teachers.

2. One of Isaiah's sons.

3. He went with Paul on a missionary journey.

4. A Jewish ruler.

5. Governor of Syria.

6. An angel.

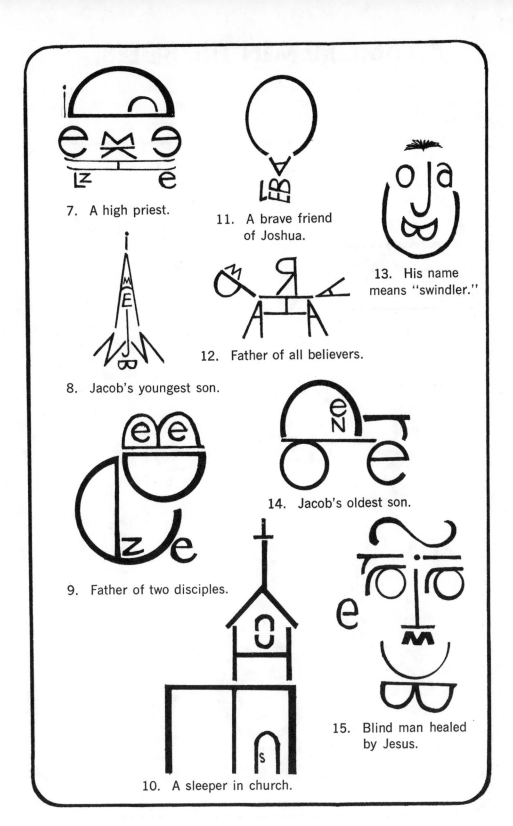

7. A high priest.

11. A brave friend of Joshua.

13. His name means "swindler."

12. Father of all believers.

8. Jacob's youngest son.

14. Jacob's oldest son.

9. Father of two disciples.

15. Blind man healed by Jesus.

10. A sleeper in church.

# 87. MORE MEN IN THE BIBLE

Hidden in these pictures are the letters in the names of some men in the Bible. One clue is under each picture. How many names can you unscramble without looking at the answers?

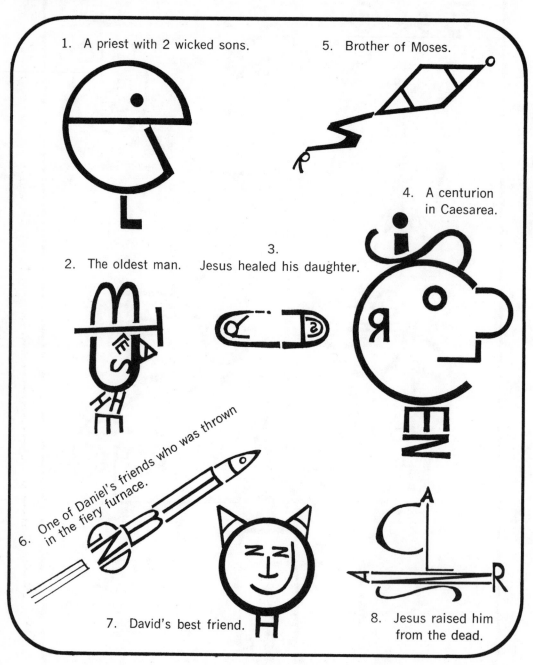

1. A priest with 2 wicked sons.

5. Brother of Moses.

4. A centurion in Caesarea.

2. The oldest man.

3. Jesus healed his daughter.

6. One of Daniel's friends who was thrown in the fiery furnace.

7. David's best friend.

8. Jesus raised him from the dead.

# 88. WOMEN IN THE BIBLE

Hidden in these pictures are the letters in the names of some ladies in the Bible. The letters may be upside down or sideways or right-side up. One clue is under each picture. How many names can you unscramble without looking at the answers?

1. A very wicked queen

2. A lady general

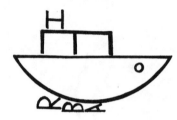

3. The mother of a very wise king

4. The sister of Moses

5. The mother of twins

6. A tentmaker

7. A Christian grandmother

8. The mother of Isaac

# 89. MORE WOMEN IN THE BIBLE

Hidden in these pictures are the letters in the names of some women in the Bible. One clue is under each picture. How many names can you unscramble without looking at the answers?

1. An old prophetess.

2. Mother of Moses.

3. One of Jesus' best friends.

4. A deaconess at Corinth.

5. The wicked wife of Herod.

6. Mother of John the Baptist.

7. Mother of the last judge in Israel.

10. One of David's wives.

8. Woman who hid two spies.

11. A betrayer.

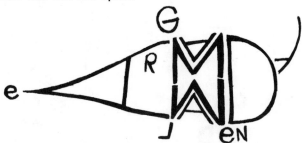

9. First woman to see Jesus after His resurrection.

12. A young dancer.

# 90. BIBLE PEOPLE STACK-A-WORD

Use the names of these Bible people to finish this puzzle.

| | | |
|---|---|---|
| LEVI | ABEL | JOB |
| MARK | LOIS | MOSES |
| RUTH | OBED | ABRAM |
| MARY | NOAH | ISAAC |
| ADAM | EHUD | SIMON |
| PAUL | ASA | JESUS |
| SAUL | LOT | TITUS |
| SETH | ELI | DAVID |
| SHEM | HAM | RHODA |
| CAIN | DAN | LABAN |

# 91. A CIRCLE OF BIBLE PEOPLE

Some Bible people had very short names — only four letters. Make a circle of these names, putting one letter in each of the squares. The last letter of the first name is the same as the first letter of the second name, and so on until the circle is completed. See how many names you can guess without looking up the Bible reference.

1. Adam's second son (Gen. 4:2)
2. Jacob's first wife (Gen. 29:23)
3. Father of a spy (Num. 13:5)
4. Father of one who rebuilt city walls (Neh. 3:2)
5. Grandfather of Zechariah (Zech. 1:1)
6. Son of Ruth and Boaz (Ruth 4:17)
7. Saul's chief herdsman (I Sam. 21:7)
8. A troublemaker in Shechem (Judg. 9:26-41)
9. Grandmother of Timothy (II Tim. 1:5)
10. Mother of Isaac (Heb. 11:11)
11. The first father (Gen. 4:1)
12. Naomi wanted this to be her name (Ruth 1:20)

# 92. FIND THE WELL

Mark is trying to decide which is the shortest path to the well so that he can take his pet goat there. He can't seem to find the right way. Can you help him?

# 93. THE LOST WHEEL

Reuben was having a chariot race with his friend when — ZIP! off came a wheel. Help him find the right wheel.

# 94. THE LOST SANDAL

Will you please help Rachel find her lost sandal?

# 95. TENT MAZE

Daniel and Ruth forgot to check the location of their tent before they went out to explore the area. Can you help them find their tent? It's the one with the striped door.

# 96. SMOKE SIGNALS #1

Can you read this smoke signal message? If you can follow the white smoke all the way up to a letter, write the letter in one of the squares above the smoke.

# 97. SMOKE SIGNALS #2

Can you read Joel's smoke signal message? If you can follow the white smoke all the way up to a letter, write the letter in one of the squares above the smoke.

# 98. A CARAVAN

How many wrong things can you find in this picture?

# 99. FIND THE MISTAKES

How many wrong things can you find in this picture?

# 100. A STREET IN OLD JERUSALEM
How many wrong things can you find in this picture?

# 101. THE FISHERMEN

These men have just come in after a long night of fishing on the Sea of Galilee. How many wrong things can you find in this picture?

# ANSWERS

## 14. PICTURE PUZZLE

Thou shalt not kill; Thou shalt not steal

## 15. STACK-A-WORD

```
         S
         H
       BEAR
         P
         H
         E
       H R
     DAVID
         R
       PSALM
         I
         O
    ANOINTED
    B
    S   SHEEP
    A   T
  SOLOMON
    O N S
    M TEMPLE
          I K
          N I
        GIANT
            G
```

## 4. STACK-A-WORD

```
       S
  CREATION
R      A
E EARTH      S
A    SE      A
T    DAY C   N
U      V LAND
R      E   T W
E    NIGHT   A
S    S   LIGHT
         E R E
           A R
       ANIMALS
       A   SEAS
    WOMAN     N
      O       T
      O   BIRDS
    SUN
    N
  WHALES
      K
    F E
  INSECTS
  S
  H
```

## 6. JUST FOR FUN

And God made two great lights,
The greater light to rule the day,
and the lesser light to rule the night:
he made the stars also.

## 8. THE TEN PLAGUES

fish, frogs, flies, lice, hail, vines, fig
trees, locusts, caterpillars, herbs, cloud,
fire, quails, rock, river.

## 12. CLIMBING THROUGH THE JORDAN VALLEY

| | |
|---|---|
| 1. Ard | 18. Ham |
| 2. Dan | 19. Methuselah |
| 3. Namaan | 20. Hosea |
| 4. Naphtali | 21. Aaron |
| 5. Issachar | 22. Nun |
| 6. Reuben | 23. Nehemiah |
| 7. Noah | 24. Hoshea |
| 8. Hushim | 25. Asa |
| 9. Manesseh | 26. Abraham |
| 10. Haggai | 27. Moses |
| 11. Isaac | 28. Samuel |
| 12. Carmi | 29. Laban |
| 13. Ishmael | 30. Nathan |
| 14. Lot | 31. Nahum |
| 15. Tola | 32. Moab |
| 16. Abel | 33. Boaz |
| 17. Lamech | |

## 13. GIDEON'S ARMY

| | |
|---|---|
| grasshoppers | pitcher |
| camels | lamp (torch) |
| dog | sword |
| trumpet | |

The Lord is with thee, thou mighty man of valour (Judg. 6:12).

## 16. SOLOMON

| | |
|---|---|
| v. 4—fists | v. 26—conies |
| v. 5—shield | v. 27—locusts |
| v. 14—teeth, swords, knives | v. 28—spider |
| | v. 30—lion |
| v. 17—eye | v. 31—greyhound, he goat |
| v. 19—eagle, serpent, rock, ship | v. 32—hand, mouth |
| | v. 33—nose |
| v. 25—ants | |

## 17. THE STORY OF RUTH

Elimelech, Naomi, Mahlon, Chilion, Moab
Ruth, my
God, Mara
kinsman, Boaz, reapers, sheaves
field, glean, ears, go
buy, redeem, shoe, son, Obed, grandfather, David

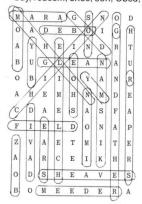

## 18. A PATIENT MAN

| | |
|---|---|
| goats | eggs |
| corn | horse |
| ass | grasshopper |
| unicorn | hawk |
| peacocks | eagle |
| ostrich | nest |

## 20. A CROSSWORD PUZZLE

## 22. NEHEMIAH

Artaxerxes, Jerusalem, walls, gates, Nehemiah
Sanballat, rulers, nobles, Samaria, fox, tower, sword,
   shield, spears, trumpet, watch, arise
horses
prayer, Ezra, ordinances, booths, pine, myrtle, oil,
   wine, corn, vessels, sanctuary, temple, sing

```
GATES     E        WATCH
      P       Z    OIL
      E    R    J     N
   S  ARTAXERXES
TOWER      R          O
R  O  SANCTUARY       R
U     R       S       D
M     D       A    F  I
P   SANBALLAT CORN
E   A     E    S X    A
T   M  NEHEMIAH       N
    A     O    I      C
  PRAYER      TEMPLE
    I     S       L I S
   ARISE          D N
     U   SING       E
  WALLS   O
      E       BOOTHS
  MYRTLE  L
      S      VESSELS
             S
```

## 23. JONAH, THE RUNAWAY

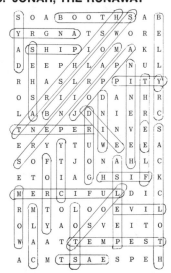

## 24. BATTLES

1—torches, trumpets, Gideon
2—Moses', Aaron, Hur
3—Jericho, marched
4—hornet
5—blinded
6—Jael, tent peg

## 26. FIND-A-WORD

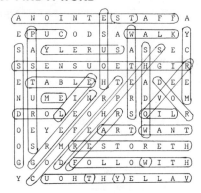

## 27. CODED MESSAGE #1

The Lord is my shepherd; I shall not want

## 28. WHO WAS AFRAID?

| | |
|---|---|
| 1 Moses | 4 Benjamin |
| 2 David | 5 Jacob |
| 3 Elijah | 6 Adam and Eve |

## 29. GOD'S WONDERFUL CARE

v. 4 feathers, wings, shield
v. 5 arrow
v. 7 hand
v. 8 eyes
v. 11 angels
v. 12 foot
v. 13 lion, adder, young lion, dragon

## 35. A MIGHTY GOD

v. 8 flower
v. 10 hand, arm
v. 11 lambs
v. 15 bucket
v. 19 chains
v. 20 tree
v. 22 circle
   grasshoppers
v. 26 eyes
v. 31 wings,
   eagles

## 36. A WALL OF LETTERS

Both young men, and maidens; old men and
children; let them praise the name of the Lord.
(Ps. 148:12, 13)

## 38. A WREATH OF LETTERS

Joy to the world, the Lord is come.

## 39. NAMES OF JESUS

anchor, rock, lion, daystar, door, lily, branch, fountain,
lamb, light, root.

## 41. THE "I AM'S" OF JESUS

bread of life; light of the world; door of the sheep;
good shepherd; resurrection and life; way, truth, life,
true vine.

## 43. A WALL OF LETTERS

Whosoever therefore shall confess me before men, him will I confess also before my Father which is in heaven. (Matt. 10:32)

## 46. GOD'S WORD

Heaven and earth shall pass away: but my words shall not pass away. (Mark 13:31)

## 47. A PROMISE FROM JESUS

I am with you alway. (Matt. 28:20)

## 53. CODED MESSAGE #2

Therefore all things whatsoever ye would that men should do to you, do ye even so to them: for this is the law and the prophets. (Matt. 7:12)

## 54. JESUS SAID

1. Peace be unto you.
2. Follow me, and I will make you fishers of men.
3. He that is of God heareth God's words.
4. If ye continue in my words, then are ye my disciples indeed.
5. He that believeth on me shall never thirst.
6. I am the bread of life, he that cometh to me shall never hunger.

## 55. THE TWELVE DISCIPLES

| | |
|---|---|
| 1. Andrew | 1. Thomas |
| 2. Simon Peter | 2. Simon the Zealot |
| 3. James | 3. Andrew |
| 4. John | 4. John |
| 5. Philip | 5. James |
| 6. Nathanael | 6. Judas Iscariot |
| 7. Matthew | 7. Philip |
| 8. Thomas | 8. Judas |
| 9. James, the Son of Alphaeus | 9. Matthew |
| | 10. Simon Peter |
| 10. Simon, the Zealot | 11. James, the Son of Alphaeus |
| 11. Judas | |
| 12. Judas Iscariot | 12. Nathanael |

## 56. CODED MESSAGE #3

I am God, and there is none else. I am God, and there is none like me, declaring the end from the beginning, and from ancient times the things that are not yet done. (Isa. 46:9-10)

## 57. JOHN, THE DISCIPLE JESUS LOVED

| | | |
|---|---|---|
| Zebedee | Jairus | Peter |
| follow | dead | Samaria |
| sons | transfigured | Philip |
| thunder | supper | First |
| John | asked | Epistle |
| fire | Mary | Revelation |
| heaven | mother | three |
| hand | disciples | sixteen |
| left | tomb | |
| king | risen | |

## 58. FIND-A-WORD

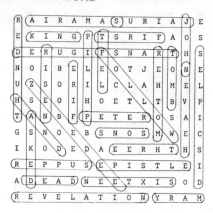

## 59. A MESSAGE FROM JOHN'S LETTER

Beloved, if God so loved us, we ought also to love one another. (I John 4:11)

## 60. CODED MESSAGE #4

Jesus said unto him, Thou shalt love the Lord thy God with all thy heart, and with all thy soul, and with all thy mind. This is the first and great commandment. And the second is like unto it, thou shalt love thy neighbor as thyself. (Matt. 22:37-39)

## 61. STEPPING STONES

Zacchaeus, Bethlehem

## 62. MONEY IN THE MOUTH

| | | |
|---|---|---|
| 1. dish | 5. dust | 9. coal |
| 2. disk | 6. dost | 10. coil |
| 3. desk | 7. cost | |
| 4. dusk | 8. coat | |

## 66. PETER

And we believe and are sure that thou art that Christ, the Son of the living God (John 6:69).

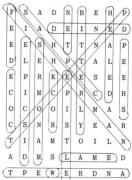

## 67. NEW TESTAMENT BOOKS

(Numbers in parenthesis refer to order of book in the New Testament)

1. Second Thessalonians (14)
2. James (20)
3. Titus (17)
4. First Corinthians (7)
5. Luke (3)
6. Romans (6)
7. Second Timothy (16)
8. The Acts (5)
9. Colossians (12)
10. Second John (24)
11. Galatians (9)
12. First Peter (21)
13. Philippians (11)
14. Hebrews (19)
15. Matthew (1)
16. Revelation (27)
17. Second Corinthians (8)
18. Mark (2)
19. Third John (25)
20. First Thessalonians (13)
21. Jude (26)
22. First Timothy (15)
23. Philemon (18)
24. John (4)
25. Ephesians (10)
26. First John (23)
27. Second Peter (22)

## 68. CODED MESSAGE #5

But thou, O man of God, flee these things; and follow after righteousness, godliness, faith, love, patience, meekness. Fight the good fight of faith, lay hold on eternal life. (1 Tim. 6:11-12)

## 69. BIBLE QUESTIONS

1. who can be against us
2. change his spots
3. mouth
4. one hour
5. keeper
6. not do what I tell you
7. betray the Son of man with a kiss
8. faith
9. touched me
10. without a preacher

## 70. DIGIT DIAMONDS

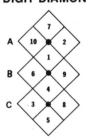

## 71. TWO MESSAGES

Blessed is the man that trusteth in the Lord (Jer. 17:7).

This is my commandment, That ye love one another, as I have loved you. (John 15:12)

## 72. LITTLE THINGS

1—stones; 2—mote; 3—mites; 4—hairs; 5—mustard seed; 6—tongue

## 73. GOD SAID THIS

He shall call upon me, and I will answer him: I will be with him in trouble; I will deliver him, and honor him (Ps. 91:15).

## 74. GOOD ADVICE

Be ye doers of the word, and not hearers only. (James 1:22)

## 75. GOLDEN OBJECTS

1. crown
2. earring
3. bowl
4. cup
5. rings
6. bed
7. apple
8. feathers
9. bell
10. spoon
11. mice
12. scepter
13. candlestick
14. chain
15. tongs

## 76. BIBLE BEEHIVE

1. And BE ye KIND one to another.
2. BE ye therefore FOLLOWERS of GOD, as dear children.
3. BE STRONG in the Lord.
4. Commit thy works unto the LORD, and thy THOUGHTS shall BE ESTABLISHED.
5. And BE ye THANKFUL.
6. That ye STUDY to BE QUIET.
7. BE thou an EXAMPLE of the believers, in word, in conversation.
8. BE not WISE in thine own EYES; fear the LORD, and DEPART from evil.
9. BE CAREFUL for nothing; but in every thing by prayer and supplication with thanksgiving let your requests BE MADE KNOWN unto God.
10. ASK, and it shall BE GIVEN you; seek and ye shall find; knock, and it shall BE OPENED unto you.
11. For where your TREASURE is, there will your HEART BE also.

## 77. WHERE DID THEY LIVE?

Lot—tent
Noah—large boat
Man with unclean spirits —among tombstones
Moses—palace

Adam and Eve—garden
John the Baptist—desert
Lazarus—outside a rich man's gate
Samuel—temple

## 78. RIDES

Abraham's servant —camel
Balaam—ass
Jesus—colt
Elijah—fiery chariot
Paul—basket and rope

Noah—ark
Moses—basket of bulrushes
The paralytic—bed
Pharoah's army—horses and chariots

## 79. WHAT DID THEY EAT?

John the Baptist —locusts
Esau—pottage
Eve—fruit

The disciples —kernels of corn
David—showbread
The Israelites

## 80. I-A-H NAMES

1. Nehemiah
2. Ahaziah
3. Amaziah
4. Isaiah
5. Hezekiah
6. Azariah
7. Zedekiah
8. Jeremiah
9. Obadiah
10. Zechariah
11. Josiah
12. Melchiah

### E-L NAMES

1. Samuel
2. Ishmael
3. Gamaliel
4. Bethuel
5. Bazaleel
6. Daniel

## 81. COUNTING SHEEP

1. 6
2. 12
3. 5
4. 5
5. 2
6. 3
7. 3

## 82. LET'S GO FISHING

| | | |
|---|---|---|
| 1. 1 | 5. 6 | 8. 1 |
| 2. 2 | 6. 2 | 9. 2 |
| 3. 2 | 7. 5 | 10. 3 |
| 4. 8 | | |

## 83. MORDECAI'S MESSAGE

Who knoweth whether thou art come to the kingdom for such a time as this?

## 84. WHO AM I?

| | | |
|---|---|---|
| 1. Peter | 4. Goliath | 7. Timothy |
| 2. Saul | 5. Mary | 8. Joseph |
| 3. Ruth | 6. Jesus | |

## 85. ANOTHER "WHO AM I?"

| | | |
|---|---|---|
| 1. Mary | 4. Jeremiah | 7. Pilate |
| 2. Absalom | 5. Namaan | 8. Titus |
| 3. Elijah | 6. Matthew | |

## 86. MEN IN THE BIBLE

| | |
|---|---|
| 1. Gamaliel | 9. Zebedee |
| 2. Mahershalalhashbaz | 10. Eutychus |
| 3. Barnabas | 11. Caleb |
| 4. Nicodemus | 12. Abraham |
| 5. Quirinius | 13. Jacob |
| 6. Gabriel | 14. Reuben |
| 7. Melchizedek | 15. Bartimaeus |
| 8. Benjamin | |

## 87. MORE MEN IN THE BIBLE

| | | |
|---|---|---|
| 1. Eli | 4. Cornelius | 7. Jonathan |
| 2. Methuselah | 5. Aaron | 8. Lazarus |
| 3. Jairus | 6. Abednego | |

## 88. WOMEN IN THE BIBLE

| | | |
|---|---|---|
| 1. Jezebel | 4. Miriam | 7. Lois |
| 2. Deborah | 5. Rebekah | 8. Sarah |
| 3. Bathsheba | 6. Priscilla | |

## 89. MORE WOMEN IN THE BIBLE

| | | |
|---|---|---|
| 1. Anna | 7. Hannah |
| 2. Jochebed | 8. Rahab |
| 3. Martha | 9. Mary Magdalene |
| 4. Phoebe | 10. Abigail |
| 5. Herodias | 11. Delilah |
| 6. Elizabeth | 12. Salome |

## 90. BIBLE PEOPLE STACK-A-WORD

```
              P  H
            ASA
             U  M
          SAUL
   SETH     E
ABRAM
   U
   T         ADAM
 RHODA        A
     B      MARY
     E     O  K
 J E  LOIS       D
NOAH L  B  ELI  LABAN
B U E  E  S  SIMON
   DAVID     A  T
     I       A  T
            CAIN
              T
              U
           JESUS
```

## 91. A CIRCLE OF BIBLE PEOPLE

| | | |
|---|---|---|
| 1. Abel | 7. Doeg |
| 2. Leah | 8. Gaal |
| 3. Hori | 9. Lois |
| 4. Imri | 10. Sara |
| 5. Iddo | 11. Adam |
| 6. Obed | 12. Mara |

## 96. SMOKE SIGNALS #1

God is love.

## 97. SMOKE SIGNALS #2

Jesus saves.